CREATIVE
CORRESPONDENCE

MICHAEL & JUDY JACOBS

here's some
seattle paper ephemera
for your mailart
see inside

NORTH LIGHT BOOKS
CINCINNATI, OHIO
www.artistsnetwork.com

To our dads: Jake and Pops, we miss you!

Arthur L. Pilon 1915–2001   M.E. (Jake) Jacobs 1920–2001

Creative Correspondence. © 2003 by Michael and Judy Jacobs. Manufactured in China. All rights reserved. The patterns in this book are for the personal use of the reader. By permission of the author and the publisher, they may be either hand traced or photocopied to make single copies, but under no circumstances may they be resold or republished. No other part of this book may be reproduced in any form or by any electronic or mechanical means, including information storage and retrieval systems, without permission in writing from the publisher, except by a reviewer, who may quote brief passages in a review. Published by North Light Books, an imprint of F&W Publications, Inc., 4700 East Galbraith Road, Cincinnati, Ohio 45236. (800) 289-0963. First edition.

Other fine North Light Books are available from your local bookstore, art supply store or direct from the publisher.
07   06   05   04   03   5   4   3   2   1

Library of Congress Cataloging-in-Publication Data
Jacobs, Michael
      Creative Correspondence / by Michael & Judy Jacobs.
         p. cm.
      Includes index.
      ISBN 1-58180-317-6 (pbk. : alk. paper)
      1. Paper work. 2. Mail art. 3. Handicraft. I. Jacobs, Judy. II. Title.
TT870 .J324 2003
745.54—dc21

2002041084

Editor: Liz Koffel Schneiders
Designer: Stephanie Strang
Layout Artist: Kathy Gardner
Production Coordinator: Michelle Ruberg
Photography: Christine Polomsky and Al Parrish

metric conversion chart

TO CONVERT	TO	MULTIPLY BY
Inches	Centimeters	2.54
Centimeters	Inches	0.4
Feet	Centimeters	30.5
Centimeters	Feet	0.03
Yards	Meters	0.9
Meters	Yards	1.1
Sq. Inches	Sq. Centimeters	6.45
Sq. Centimeters	Sq. Inches	0.16
Sq. Feet	Sq. Meters	0.09
Sq. Meters	Sq. Feet	10.8
Sq. Yards	Sq. Meters	0.8
Sq. Meters	Sq. Yards	1.2
Pounds	Kilograms	0.45
Kilograms	Pounds	2.2
Ounces	Grams	28.4
Grams	Ounces	0.04

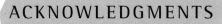

about THE AUTHORS

Michael Jacobs is Art Director of The Creative Zone and a full-time book artist and instructor who has worked in mixed media and sculpture for over thirty years. For eight of those years, he operated a design studio specializing in paper engineering, props and signage. His work has been published in many books and periodicals, and exhibited at the Art Directors Club in New York and in numerous galleries. In 1990 he designed and fabricated the World's Largest Photo Album for the Kodak Goodwill Games, and has been creating sculptural books ever since. His artist books are in private collections across America, and he teaches papercraft and book-arts workshops throughout the United States and Canada.

Judy Jacobs, M.A., is Creative Director of The Creative Zone and has long divided her time between writing, teaching and performing. Over the years her feature articles have appeared in newspapers and trade publications, including *RubberStampMadness*, *Rubber Stampin' Retailer*, *Papercrafters* and *The Studio*. Her teaching repertoire includes public speaking, rubber stamping and papercraft, and creative playing around. Passionate about theatre, she has directed and produced twelve shows, acted in numerous productions, performed voice-overs for radio and TV, and spoken to business groups about creativity in the workplace. Her artist books and cards have been published in several books and periodicals.

Visit the Jacobs' Web site at www.thecreativezone.com

ACKNOWLEDGMENTS

With joy and gratitude, we thank the following people:

- Liz Koffel Schneiders, our editor and fellow papercrafter, for her professional attention to detail.
- Christine Polomsky, our photographer, for her expertise and positive attitude which made the photo shoot so fun.
- Stephanie Strang, our designer, for making us look so good.
- Vesta Abel, for paving the way.
- Heidi Mirka, whose generosity of spirit (and studio space) made it possible for us to complete this book.

- Our families, for support of all kinds over the years.
- Barbara McBeath, whose faith in us is constant.
- Our students, who keep taking classes so we don't have to get real jobs.
- Lunelle Chapin, who taught Judy the value of high journalistic standards.
- Marlene Teel, who called Michael an artist for the first time, and believed it.

TABLE OF
CONTENTS

Jumping In

Pocket Surprises

More Fun With Folds

Magic Up Your Sleeves

The Envelope Please

Introduction

Years ago we entered the exciting world of **mail art**, corresponding with other mail artists around the country and overseas. Our mailbox was a constant source of anticipation and surprise. And then, along came e-mail, creating instant communication with no travel time and no postage. Now, even we who make our living working with paper, reluctantly resort to sending e-mail more and more. However, we continue to send decorative mail to friends and family because we know the excitement it generates on the receiving end.

Our goal with this book is to make it possible for people who don't have a lot of time (isn't that everyone?) to make and send decorative mail. We show how easy it is to turn a piece of paper into correspondence art: a tactile messenger of good will, a colorful container for your latest news. The projects are simple yet spectacular, requiring a few basic tools, a little measuring, and some folding and cutting. The most difficult part will be choosing which beautiful paper to use with what project. The easy part will

be changing the dimensions of the foldnotes, sleeves and inserts
so you can mix and match them to suit your fancy.

And because our favorite slogan is **Reduce, Reuse,
Recycle,** we've made some of the samples in this book from used
paper. Make yours from used or new paper, or creatively combine
them. Then, add your personal touch quickly and easily with rubber
stamping, collage, colored pencils and more. We give you lots of
visual ideas and a few tips along the way.

We hope you have just as much fun as we do making these
projects. May you be inspired to use our ideas as a starting point for
your own creative correspondence.

Michael Jacobs AND *Judy Jacobs*

Performance
★
8 p.m. curtain
Act Now!
POSTE

SEATTLE
3-d
kinda
GUY
W.A.

Genuine

Genuine

#120 OF 20

DIVINE
DISGUSTING

?

UNOFFICIAL
dear mom!

Tools and Materials

✉ You can create wonderful correspondence art with as few as ten tools in your basic tool kit. With these tools, you can make all of the projects in this book. Everything else listed in "Other Fun Stuff" is just frosting on your cake.

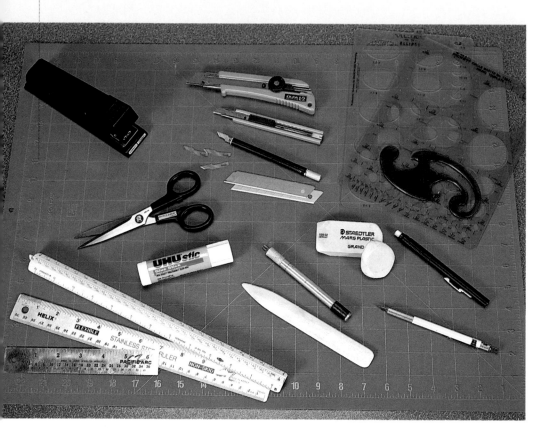

mechanical pencil We strongly recommend a 0.5mm pencil with 2H lead. The hard, narrow lead makes a thin, non-smearing line, which is best for accuracy.

rulers Rulers come in different lengths and materials, and believe it or not, they are meant to be used for different jobs. For cutting, start with a 12" (30cm) metal ruler, with or without cork on the back side to keep it from sliding around. For measuring, buy a plastic three-sided architectural ruler with a $1/16$" scale—this means one of its sides has inches divided into sixteenths. We use this scale for all our projects.

knives Craft knives come in different sizes and are best for cutting paper. Utility knives, which are larger and have a heavy-duty blade, are better for cutting heavier paper, cardstock and board. Look for one with snap-off blades.

scissors We have two pairs of scissors, one large and one small. Scissors are useful for cutting curves; however, we always cut straight lines with a knife and ruler.

self-healing cutting mat Cutting mats come in different sizes. Small mats are great for traveling; however, if you're going to get only one, a medium size or larger is much more practical.

bone folder Bone folders come in handy for a number of jobs, including scoring and creasing. If the scoring end is too thick, it can be shaped with a fine grade of sandpaper to the desired thickness. You can also make your own scoring tool out of a knife handle and a jumbo paperclip (see page 14).

glue We recommend the Uhu glue stick, which is acid-free, goes on smoothly, and is water-soluble so it washes off easily. Stick to the medium or large size for the best deal.

stapler For binding, a standard hinged stapler is as complicated as we get in these correspondence projects.

templates and French curves Plastic templates and curves come in all shapes and sizes. These are a must for transferring circles, ovals and curves quickly and easily. We use them for windows and customized flaps.

erasers Look for white vinyl erasers, which erase your pencil marks and lines cleanly, with minimal particle build-up. We like the long, tubular erasers that come in a penlike holder.

OTHER FUN STUFF

mouth atomizer This is a fun little gadget once referred to as the poor man's airbrush. Use it to create a spattered pattern on the front of a foldnote (see page 29). Cheap and portable, it's found in art supply stores.

brayer A brayer is a roller with a handle, often used to roll paint or ink onto paper. For our brayering technique shown on page 17, you'll need a softer brayer that comes apart so you can wrap the roller with rubber bands.

decorative scissors and cutters These are perfect for creating fun decorative edges on your paper. Olfa, Fiskars and other companies also make decorative cutters that look and act like mini pizza cutters. Or dig out those old pinking shears.

punches These handy little gadgets can create beautiful corners on your paper, or you can punch out fun shapes for more decoration and embellishment.

tweezers Tweezers come in handy for picking up and positioning smaller pieces of paper, especially when you have glue on your fingers.

acrylic paints and brushes Acrylics are pigment paints that come in myriad vibrant colors. Lightfast and versatile, they can be used as is, or watered down and used as a wash. We suggest getting at least two acrylic brushes: one small and one wide.

markers We use double-ended markers with a fine point and a bullet point to address envelopes, outline labels, add bits of color, draw, etc.

crayons Wax crayons are great for adding quick color to your projects and for creating crayon-resist papers.

colored pencils We use colored pencils all the time for quick embellishing. The softer pencils color in larger areas more easily, but tend to wear down faster. Both soft and hard pencils make great squiggles.

Prismacolor Art Stix are Michael's favorite color tool. They are richly pigmented colored pencils without the wood. Use flat for a wide swath of color, or hold like a crayon to add quick squiggles.

rubber stamps Rubber stamps are tailor-made for correspondence art. We use a combination of retail stamps, hand-carved stamps, and stamps we've had made from clip art. (See page 95 for a complete list of stamp credits.)

ink pads Ink pads are one of the quickest ways to add color to your art. Use with rubber stamps, or stamp the ink pad itself directly onto the paper. Cool!

Dye-based ink is thin, dries fast and cleans up easily. Pigment ink is thicker, does not dry on coated paper, is great for embossing and resists fading.

paint scrapers You can buy paint scrapers made specifically for creating patterns in wet paint or paste. You'll find them in craft stores and paint stores.

newsprint pad A large pad of newsprint is the perfect protection for your work surface whenever you stamp or paint.

squirt bottle A must for adding water to your paint a little at a time, or for wetting your stamping-off towel.

double-stick tape Look for the kind on a roll with peel-off backing so you can work with one sticky side at a time. Excellent for closing envelopes, sleeves and foldnotes, and for attaching inserts to your correspondence projects.

sealing wax and seals Popular in the Victorian Age when correspondence was queen, sealing wax and decorative seals can be found in stationery and rubber stamp stores. What a great finishing touch for a beautiful foldnote!

Postal Regulations

Almost all of the projects in this book (with the exception, perhaps, of the Letter in a Bag project on page 70) can be safely mailed at the basic letter rate. If you design your own correspondence projects, or plan to adapt any in this book to a different size or shape, we highly recommend asking your local post office for a list of standard rates and dimensions.

The United States Postal Service also offers a Mail Dimensional Standards Template. Brilliantly designed and easy to use, this plastic template indicates the acceptable height-to-length ratios for first-class and single-piece third-class mail weighing one ounce or less. Also included are minimum and maximum postcard sizes and a cut-out slot for measuring thickness. It makes sizing mail a cinch—and it's free!

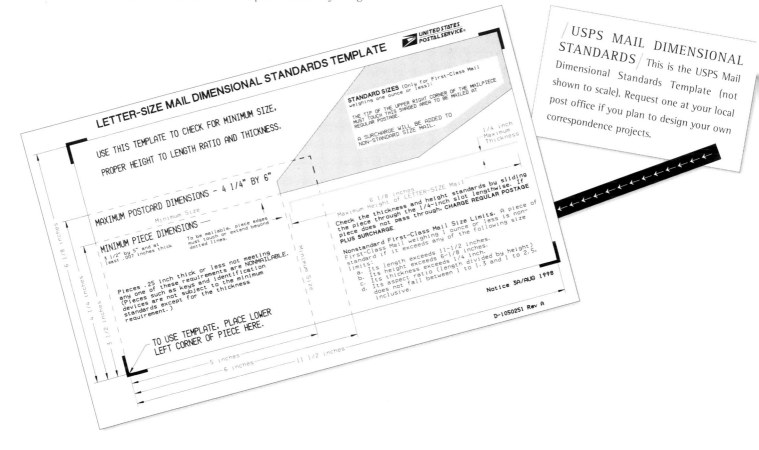

USPS MAIL DIMENSIONAL STANDARDS / This is the USPS Mail Dimensional Standards Template (not shown to scale). Request one at your local post office if you plan to design your own correspondence projects.

Here are a few guidelines for mailing correspondence art in the United States:

Postcards: Minimum size is 3½" x 5" (8.9cm x 12.7cm) and at least .007 inches thick. Maximum size is 4¼" x 6" (10.8cm x 15.2cm).

Letters: Minimum size is 3½" x 5" (8.9cm x 12.7cm) and at least .007 inches thick. Maximum size is 6⅛" x 11½" (15.5cm x 29.2cm) and no more than one-quarter inch (6mm) thick.

Be sure to check the height-to-length ratio of your letter. Some mail within this range is either too tall or too long to qualify as standard and will need additional postage.

For more information on postal rates and dimensions, you can visit the following Web sites:

United States: www.usps.com
United Kingdom: www.consignia-online.com
Canada: www.canadapost.ca

Choosing the Right Paper

Paper has definitely come a long way since its invention in China in A.D. 105. The abundance of types, weights, textures and colors is enough to boggle the mind. Where the heck do you start?

You start by keeping it simple. Most of our projects use commercial papers. Accessible, affordable and colorful, these papers are sold by the individual sheet so you can try them out before going on a buying spree. The remaining projects are made from hand-decorated or used papers.

Bond and Text Weight Papers

Think of papers used for stationery, photocopies and typewriters (oops! we mean printers). You can buy these papers individually or by the ream (500 sheets).

Decorative Papers

Any thin decorative paper you like is great for embellishing correspondence art. Think of wrapping paper, marbled paper, scrapbook papers, colored and designer tissue paper, Japanese lace papers, etc.

Cardstock

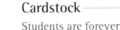

Students are forever e-mailing to say, "What the heck is cardstock? My store didn't know what I was talking about." Simply put, cardstock is just heavier paper. It's what greeting cards, business cards and postcards are usually made from (*cards*, get it?) Cardstock ranges in weight from 65 lb. to 110 lb. (140gsm to 235gsm); anything over 110 lb. (235gsm) and we're talking cardboard or mat board.

You can buy large sheets of cardstock and cut them down to size, or purchase a ream of 250 letter-sized sheets. When buying by the ream, read the end label. For our projects, when the materials list says cardstock, anything from 65 lb. to 80 lb. (140gsm to 170gsm) will be perfect.

Used Papers

Seattle, where we live, is one of the most recycle-conscious cities in the country. Everywhere you go you see the words *Reduce, Reuse, Recycle*. Used paper is our favorite source for mail art. It's abundant, it's free, and it comes in a humongous variety of colors, sizes, printed designs and textures. You probably have some of these around the house even as we speak: old maps and atlases, calendar pages, wrapping paper, junk mail, shopping bags, posters, brochures, envelopes, paper promotions, colorful newsprint and architectural drawings. Local printers can also be a great source of paper and cardstock. They often sell or give away leftovers from print jobs.

Basic Paper Techniques

THE BEST WAY TO MEASURE, SCORE AND CUT PAPER

The simple truth is—it takes no more time to be precise when measuring and cutting than it does to be sloppy. In fact, these few techniques will make your life in paper easier and will save you time in the long run.

Honest. Even students with extensive papercraft experience have told us they improved their skills with these techniques.

① CHOOSE A GOOD RULER

The best ruler for measuring is a triangular architectural ruler (shown at bottom). Its angled surface has skinnier lines which rest right on the paper, so you can accurately transfer measurements to your paper.

When measuring, make sure your ruler is lined up properly and parallel to the top and bottom edges of the paper. Be sure you know where the zero point is before you begin measuring. In this photo, the top ruler's zero point is right at the end of the ruler, but the middle ruler's zero point is set in from the end.

② MEASURE AND MARK THE TOP OF YOUR PAPER

Whenever you need to draw, score or cut a line, first align your ruler properly, then measure over from the left and make small pencil marks. First mark your measurements toward the top of your paper, to indicate any lines. If using a metal ruler, tilt the ruler up to simulate an architectural ruler for greater accuracy.

③ MARK THE BOTTOM OF YOUR PAPER

Now do the same thing at the bottom of your paper, measuring from the left and making small pencil marks.

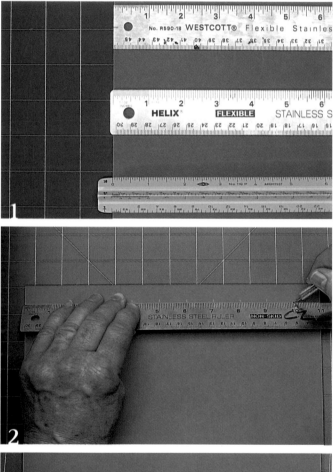

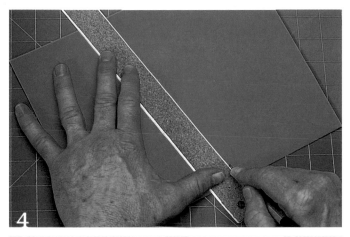

4 POSITION YOUR TOOL

After you've made marks at the top and bottom of your cardstock, stab the very center of the bottom mark with your pencil (or knife or scoring tool if you are cutting or folding) and slide the lower end of a metal ruler firmly against it.

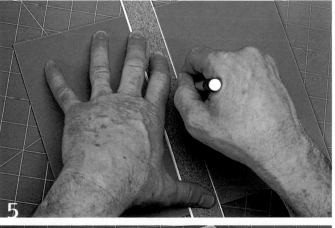

5 ALIGN THE RULER WITH THE MARKS

Now slide the top end of the ruler to the top mark, then back off just a hair to account for the thickness of your pencil, knife or scoring tool. With practice, this stabbing and sliding will increase accuracy and save you time.

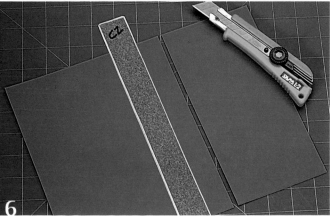

6 CUT OR SCORE YOUR PAPER

Press down firmly on your ruler. Draw the pencil, scoring tool or knife blade toward you, keeping it at a steady angle. If you are cutting thicker paper or cardstock, use a heavy knife and make several swipes with the blade.

HOW TO MAKE GREAT FOLDS

Cardstock and heavier paper fold easily and cleanly when they have been scored first. When you score your paper with a bone folder or a scoring tool, you compress the fibers so they will bend more readily.

Follow the basic measuring guidelines on page 12 to make your scoring accurate. The object is to score down the very center of your pencil marks, so adjust your ruler placement to account for the thickness of your scoring tool.

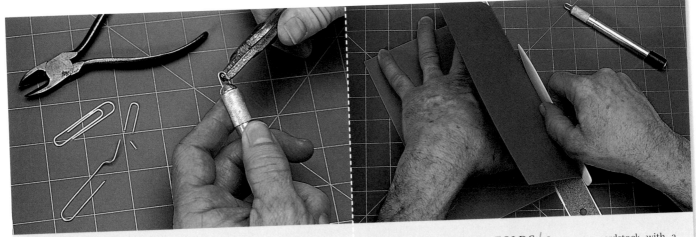

/MAKING YOUR OWN SCORING TOOL/ Here's how to create our preferred scoring tool. Unfold a large paper clip and snip off the smaller inside rounded end, about ³/₄" (2cm) long, with wire cutters. Lightly hammer the cut ends to flatten slightly. With your pliers, push the cut ends into the open end of a medium craft knife handle, then tighten the chuck. This lifetime tool is ideal for scoring cardstock and heavy paper.

/MAKING CLEAN FOLDS/ Score your cardstock with a ruler and scoring tool. Keeping your ruler in place, run your bone folder along the crease on the back side of the cardstock. The cardstock will bend easily along the edge of the ruler. (This only works if you score with the ruler placed cork side up.)

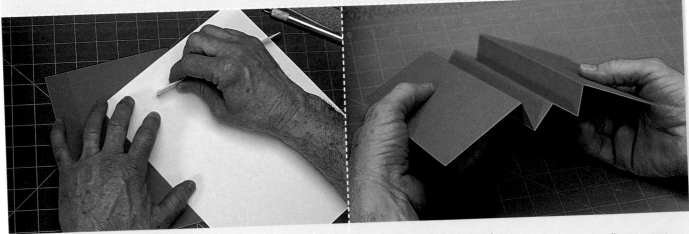

/CREASING YOUR FOLDS/ When you fold cardstock, line up the edges, then lay a clean sheet of scrap paper on top of the fold to protect it. Crease heavily with your bone folder.

/TYPES OF FOLDS/ Folds are referred to as valley or mountain folds. A score line made on the front of your cardstock creates a valley fold. A score line made on the back of the cardstock creates a mountain fold.

How Grain Direction Affects Folds

Machine-made paper, cardstock and cardboard all have a grain direction. This simply means that the fibers from which the paper is made all lie in one direction. Why is this important? Because paper folded against the grain—across the direction of the fibers—is weaker, tends to crack, and will not lie as flat. And we wouldn't want that to happen to you.

For the best results as you make these projects, watch for notations in the materials lists and tip boxes stating whether your paper should be *grain short* (with the grain running parallel to the width of the paper), or *grain long* (with the grain direction running parallel to the length). When specified, this indicates the correct grain direction after you've cut out your project papers or cardstock. Trim your paper accordingly and your folds will be crisp and lie flat. However, take these directions with a "grain of salt"—these projects will look good and function well even if you occasionally go "against the grain."

If you like to buy paper by the ream, the label will sometimes indicate the grain direction. If the *11* on a label of 8½" x 11" paper is underlined, then the paper is grain long. If the *8½* is underlined, then the paper is grain short. When in doubt, test your paper using the techniques below, and always try to crease your paper in the same direction as the grain.

Quick Tricks for Determining Grain Direction

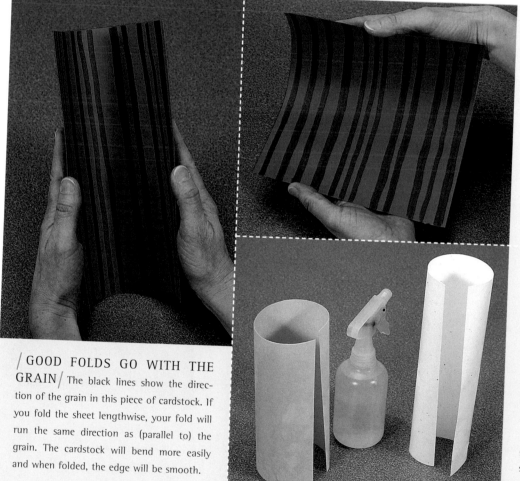

/ WEAK FOLDS GO AGAINST THE GRAIN/ If you bend the same piece of cardstock across the width, you will feel more resistance because you are bending against the direction of the grain. Your folded edge will be weaker and visually rough.

/ TRY THE SPRAY TEST/ If you can't tell the grain direction by feeling the resistance, then lightly spray your paper with a fine mist of water and see which way it curls—it will curl around the direction of the grain.

Both pieces of cardstock at left are 8½" x 11" (21.6cm x 28cm). The curled blue cardstock is grain short and the white cardstock is grain long.

/ GOOD FOLDS GO WITH THE GRAIN/ The black lines show the direction of the grain in this piece of cardstock. If you fold the sheet lengthwise, your fold will run the same direction as (parallel to) the grain. The cardstock will bend more easily and when folded, the edge will be smooth.

Decorating Paper by Hand

With the incredible choice of decorative papers on the market, why would anyone spend time decorating her own? Because it's easy and fun and creative and . . . well, some of us need to express ourselves this way. And, like the correspondence projects coming up, hand-decorated papers can be prepared in quantity and customized to fit the occasion. The following techniques are super simple, yet the results are simply super!

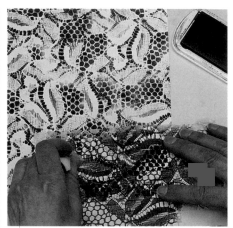

Stamping with Netting Wadded-up nylon netting, such as this bath sponge, creates a beautiful, delicate pattern when used as a stamp. Choose light-colored or metallic pigment inks for best results on black paper. For a fun variation, try stamping with bubble wrap or plastic wrap.

Texture Rubbing with Wax Resist Almost anything can be used as a rubbing surface to create interesting texture. We use crayons to create a waxed rubbing of a piece of textured vinyl wall covering, then paint over it with a wash of watered-down acrylic paint. The wax resists the paint for a beautiful two-tone surface effect.

Lace Stencils Create beautiful lace paper by stamping ink through a piece of lace with a make-up sponge. We started with white paper and moved a small piece of lace around the paper. Better yet, find a piece of lace larger than your paper and tape it down for quicker results.

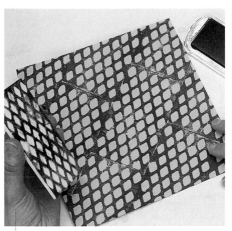

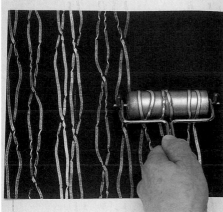

Foam Tray Stamping Save textured foam trays from the grocery store and cut out shapes to use as texture stamps. Here, we stamped a diagonal pattern on yellow paper. You can also trace your own patterns into a foam plate with a ballpoint pen.

Rubber Band Brayering We use ordinary household rubber bands twisted around a soft rubber brayer to create a simple line pattern. Roll the brayer over a metallic ink pad. Silver ink layered on black turns this paper into a rich dimensional texture.

Apple Printing Firm fruits and vegetables such as apples and potatoes make wonderful prints. Begin by stamping a light background color in a random pattern, turning the apple as you go. Stamp over the first layer in a contrasting color. Shaped wooden blocks also work well with this technique.

EASY PASTE PAPER

Paste paper usually involves a bit of preparation, like following a recipe and cooking the paste. This is why we've avoided it in the past, and why we're so excited about this recipe—there's no cooking! A student of Michael's gave us this art paste to try. All you do is add cold water, stir, and let it sit for 15 minutes. Now, that's our kind of cooking!

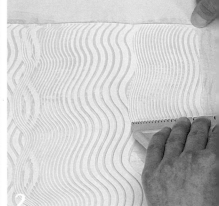

MaTeRiaLS NEEDED

- covered container
- measuring cup
- 2 oz. (57gm) box of Ross Paper Mache Art Paste
- cold water
- small plastic containers
- acrylic paints
- stir sticks
- paper to decorate (HEAVIER IS BETTER)
- wide paint brush
- paint scrapers

❶ MIX THE PASTE
Use approximately one quarter of the bag of dry paste and add one quart (946ml) of cold water. Mix your main batch in a container with a cover and let it sit according to directions. Then, dole out smaller amounts for each color and stir a gob of acrylic paint into each one. The consistency should be that of thick buttermilk.

❷ COMB THE PASTE TO MAKE PATTERNS
Paint the first color on a sheet of paper. If it doesn't spread easily, add more water and stir well. Holding down the edge of the paper, pull your paint scraper toward you while making squiggly lines. If it's not what you want, paint over it and start again.

❸ ADD A SECOND LAYER FOR CONTRAST
When the first layer is dry, paint a second color over the first and comb through it with your paint scraper. The first layer of color will combine with the second to create interesting patterns.

For a fun variation, use colored paper and layer it with paste of a different color on top.

BUBBLE MARBLING

We tried several recipes for bubble marbling, and this one from the Scribes of Central Florida makes nice, dark bubbles. The secret ingredient is the sugar, which helps bind the coloring to the paper. A little bit goes a long way—one bottle of bubbles will decorate lots of paper. And your leftovers will be just as willing to make bubbles the following day.

❶ MIX THE BUBBLE SOLUTION
Pour some bubble solution into three small containers. Add ten to twelve drops of a different color of food coloring to each one and stir thoroughly. Add one teaspoon (5g) of sugar to each color and stir until dissolved.

❷ BLOW BUBBLES TO FILL THE BOWL
Start with your lightest color. With a straw, blow bubbles that come up higher than the edge of your bowl.

If your bubbles are too light on the paper, add more drops of food coloring.

❸ POP THE BUBBLES WITH THE PAPER
Hold your paper or cardstock over the container and gently pop the bubbles without hitting the rim of the container. Blow more bubbles and repeat the process until you have a random pattern on your paper.

Add a second or third layer, overlapping the first layer with increasingly darker colors.

MaTeRiaLS NEEDED

- bubble solution
  (FOUND IN TOY STORES)
- small bowls
- food coloring
- sugar (1 tsp. [5g] to each color)
- stir sticks
- plastic straws
- paper or cardstock to decorate

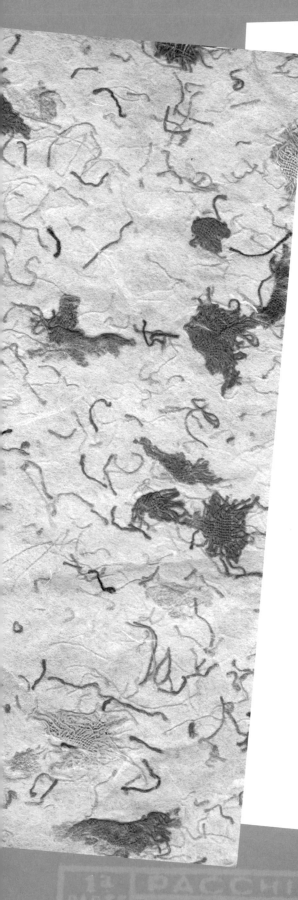

JumpingIn

The real art of creative playing around is knowing how to jump right in. Children do it every day; we big kids sometimes need a little nudging to actually do something that's… well, just for fun. Luckily, paper makes it easy to play around because it invites you to look at its beautiful colors and patterns, to feel its textures, to bend it and shape it into something more than what it is, something dimensional. And it is just this interactive nature of paper that gives us the nudge to jump in and rediscover that "child as artist."

Even if you're new to paper arts—even if you don't know a craft knife from a corner punch—all you have to do is pick up a piece of paper, make a few folds, add some colorful paper scraps, and your creative play has begun. These first few projects include stationery made from reused envelopes and handmade postcards. We'll also introduce you to *foldnotes*, a clever correspondence format in which the paper and the envelope are rolled into one. They are so simple and so fun, you'll wonder why you ever waited so long to jump in and let the good times unfold.

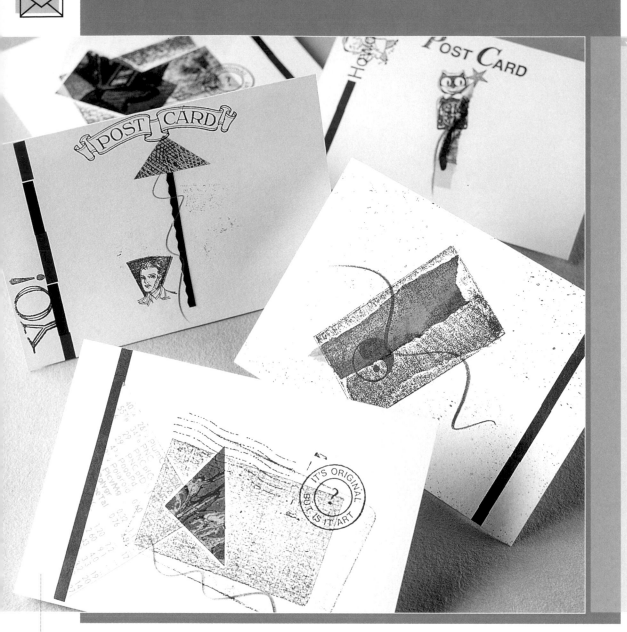

- assorted cardstock cut into pieces at least 3½" x 5" (8.9cm x 12.7cm) in size

- ruler

- scissors or craft knife

- cutting mat

- decorative paper scraps

- glue stick

- bone folder

- colored pencils

- sealing wax and seal (OPTIONAL)

- metallic ink (OPTIONAL)

Postcards are the perfect canvas for getting your feet (hands) wet in the creative process; they're too small to be intimidating. We make them up in batches, all using a similar theme, and often stamp the word *postcard* on the back to make them look official.

Artful
Collage Postcards

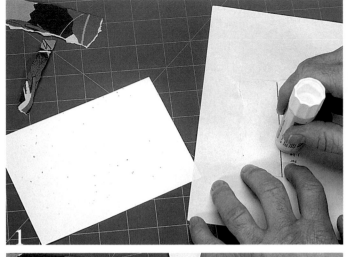

4

1 APPLY GLUE TO ASSORTED
COLLAGE PIECES

Cut your cardstock into an acceptable size for
the regular postcard rate. In the U.S. that would
be a minimum 3½" x 5" (8.9cm x 12.7cm); maximum 4¼" x 6" (10.8cm x 15.2cm). (See page 10
to find information for the U.K. and Canada.)
Grab colorful scraps of different sizes—small,
medium and large—and begin gluing.

2 PLACE THE COLLAGE ELEMENTS ON THE CARD

For a quick and colorful collage, start with the
largest piece of paper and glue it to your postcard
at an interesting angle.

3 BURNISH WELL TO FLATTEN

Lay a clean piece of scrap paper over the glued
paper and use your bone folder to smooth out any
bubbles or wrinkles.

4 ADD EXTRA DETAILS

Finish layering your paper scraps—smallest pieces
on top—and add other embellishments. In this
example you see a red ink pad stamped over the
collage, quick lines made with colored pencils, and
finally, sealing wax stamped with a seal that was
first pressed in metallic ink.

- used envelopes
- bone folder
- glue stick
- decorative paper scraps
- colorful string or yarn
- crayons or colored pencils
- rubber stamps
- ink pad

Used paper is our favorite source for mail art; it's abundant and it's free. You can make and decorate a whole stack of used envelope stationery in just a couple of hours, and either side of an envelope can be used. Keep some on hand for those occasions when you need to send a quick note.

Inside-Out
Envelope Stationery

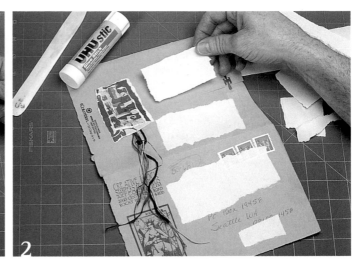

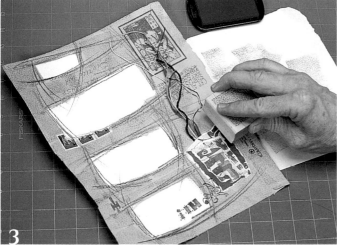

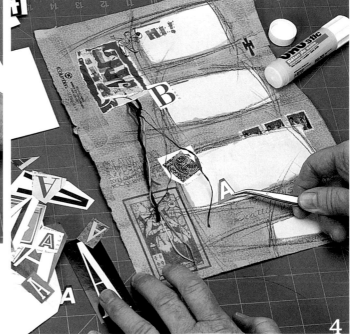

1 SLIT THE ENVELOPES OPEN

Slit the envelopes down each side with your bone folder and save for decorating.

Decide which surface of the envelope you want to use as your letter. We like the image and printing on the outside of our envelope, as well as the colorful postage stamps.

2 ADD A WRITING SPACE

Start embellishing. Paper scraps, colorful threads and yarn can be attached easily with a glue stick.

If your surface is busy, add writing areas by gluing in torn shapes of paper.

3 ADD COLOR AND TEXTURE

Outline the writing areas with crayons or colored pencils and stamp your salutation.

Next, add dimension and tie everything together by stamping a texture design over the entire surface, except for the writing areas.

4 ADD COLLAGE LETTERS

Add cut-out letters from magazines to the beginning of each writing area. Let the letters determine how you start each paragraph; or write your paragraphs first, leaving off the first letter until you know what you're saying.

COLLAGE TIP

Keep a collection of cut-out letters and words in separate envelopes, ready for collaging at a moment's notice. Save used or foreign postage stamps, too. They add exotic interest to any correspondence art.

- 8½" x 11" (21.6cm x 28cm) sheet of decorative paper
- bone folder
- ruler
- pencil
- scissors or craft knife
- cutting mat
- glue stick
- decorative paper scraps
- crayons or colored pencils
- rubber stamps
- ink pads
- double-stick tape (OPTIONAL)

What's a foldnote? It is a single sheet of letter-size paper, cleverly folded so that the stationery and envelope are one and the same. This project is a great place to discover the fun of foldnotes. Because you'll find this one quick and easy, make up multiple notes, decorate the whole bunch, and keep them handy for future occasions. When you're really crunched for time, everything will be done but the writin'!

Simple Centered Foldnote

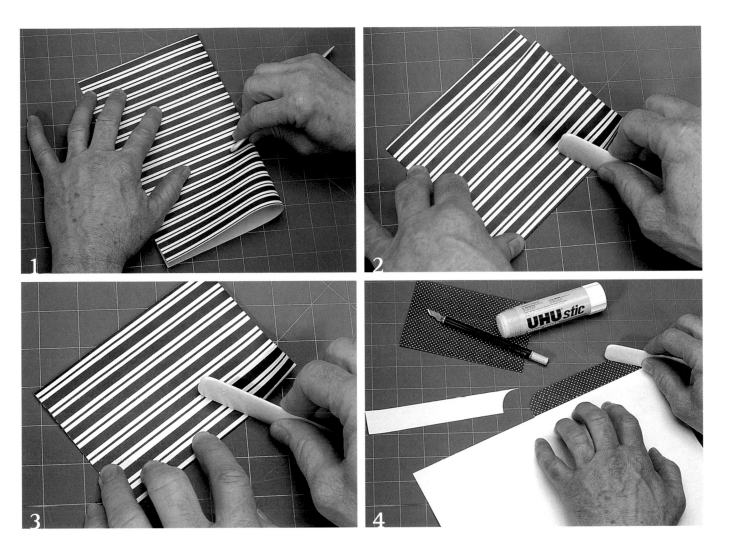

① FOLD YOUR PAPER IN HALF WIDTHWISE

With your paper horizontal and the decorative side face down, fold the paper in half across the width and crease well with a bone folder.

② FOLD THE BOTTOM UP

Fold the bottom edge up to within 1" (2.5cm) of the top and crease.

③ FOLD THE TOP DOWN

Fold the top over to create the flap and crease.

④ MAKE THE TOP FLAP

Open your note and cut away the top-left flap section. Shape the remaining flap and cover it with contrasting paper. We've covered both sides of our flap.

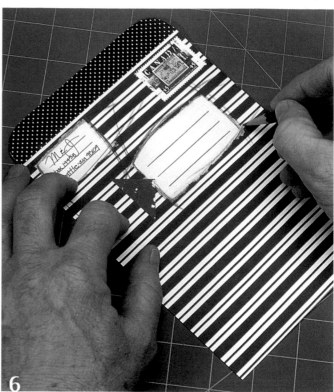

5 DECORATE AND WRITE YOUR LETTER
Decorate the inside of your foldnote with paper
scraps, crayons and rubber stamps, then write
your letter.

6 ADD AN ADDRESS LABEL
Tear out address labels from light-colored paper
and glue them to the front of the foldnote. Add
color to the edges of the labels with colored pencils
or crayons.

7 SEAL WITH A HANDMADE STICKER
Make your own decorative sticker: cut out a shape
from contrasting paper and glue it part-way onto
the flap. When you're ready to seal the note, finish
gluing the sticker closed, or use a piece of double-
stick tape.

TRY A FUN VARIATION GET CREATIVE BY ADDING
A MASKED ADDRESS LABEL TO THE OUTSIDE OF YOUR
FOLDNOTE. JUST FOLLOW THE INSTRUCTIONS ON THE
NEXT PAGE. →

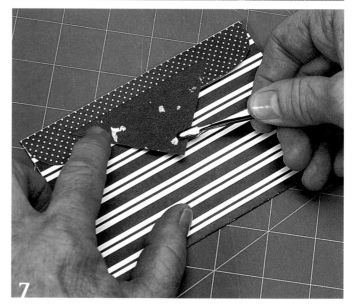

DECORATE FIRST!

We're firm believers in "Decorate first, write later!" Often, your
collage or design elements define a more interesting writing
area than if you write first and then try to squeeze in
some visual decoration.

ADDING A MASKED ADDRESS LABEL

Masking is an easy alternate way to create address labels directly on the front of a plain foldnote. By masking off an area and decorating around the mask, you define a perfect focus for the address. Fun and versatile, masks can be made in different shapes and sizes to fit the theme of any special day.

MaTeRiaLS NEEDED

- plain foldnote
- removable sticky notes
- removable tape
- scissors or craft knife
- cutting mat
- acrylic paint
- mouth atomizer (OR BLOW PEN)
- long-handled paint brush

1 MASK YOUR ADDRESS SPACES
Make a Centered Foldnote from white or colored paper. Cut sticky notes to your desired size and shape. Use the sticky edge or a small piece of removable tape to adhere the masks to the front of the note.

2 PLACE THE ATOMIZER IN THE PAINT
Put a gob of acrylic paint in a little cup, add water and mix. Open the atomizer fully and place the long skinny tube in the paint.

3 BLOW FINE SPATTERS
With the foldnote propped up in front of a large sheet of paper, hold the cup and blow through the large tube. Keep blowing as you move around to cover the entire surface.

4 ADD BIGGER SPATTERS
To create more visual interest, add bigger spatters with a paint brush and the remaining acrylic paint. Holding one hand over the paper, bring the wet brush up against the bottom of your wrist.

5 LET DRY AND ADD THE ADDRESS
Allow the spatters to dry, then remove the masks and address the note.

SAVE OUR WATER

UNITED STATES · SIX CENTS

PO BOX 19458
SEATTLE/WA
98109·1458

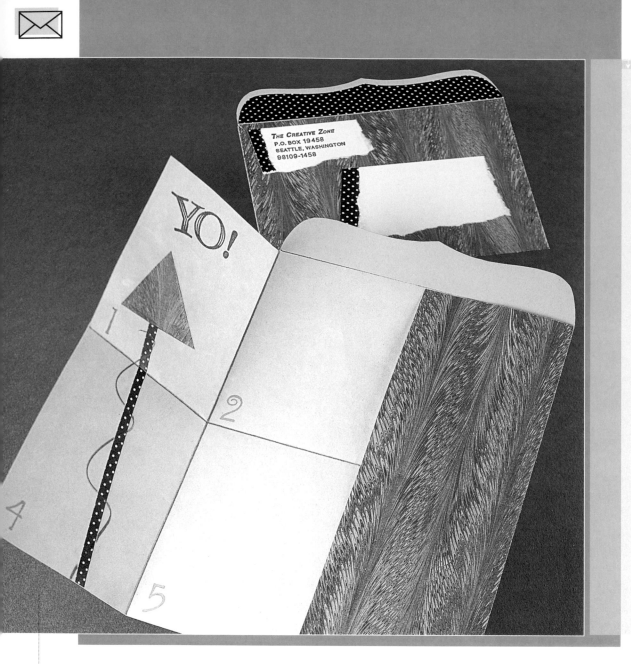

- 8½" x 11" (21.6cm x 28cm) sheet of decorative paper
- bone folder
- ruler
- pencil
- scissors or craft knife
- cutting mat
- glue stick
- decorative paper scraps
- colored pencils
- rubber stamps
- ink pads

Imitating French doors that open from the center and swing out to the sides, this foldnote (also known as a gatefold) has the added advantage of secured sides. Write your note, then enclose bits and pieces of paper ephemera like photos, tickets, recipes or newspaper clippings, knowing that everything will safely reach the intended destination.

French Door Foldnote

1 FOLD IN HALF AND PINCH THE TOP EDGE

Place your paper horizontally with the decorative side down. Bring one side over to the other as if folding in half and pinch at the top; this is the easy way to find the center without measuring.

2 FOLD THE EDGES IN TOWARD THE CENTER

Open the paper flat. Fold the left edge to the center pinch mark and crease with a bone folder. Then fold the right edge to the center and crease.

3 FOLD UP THE BOTTOM EDGE

Fold the bottom up to within 1" (2.5cm) of the top and crease.

CHANGING DIMENSIONS

You can adjust the size of this French Door Foldnote by adjusting the side flaps. When folding the sides in toward the center, simply leave a space between the two edges. The finished height of any foldnote must be at least 3½" (8.9cm) if you plan to mail it in the U.S. at the basic rate.

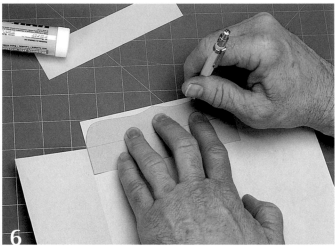

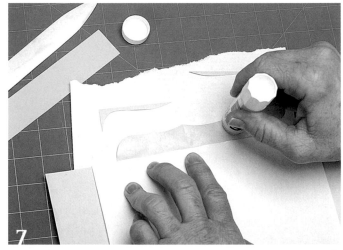

④ MAKE A TOP FLAP

Fold the top over to create a flap and crease.

⑤ CUT AWAY THE EXCESS PAPER

Open your foldnote and cut out the two upper corners with scissors or a craft knife.

⑥ SHAPE THE FLAP

Shape the remaining flap either freehand or by tracing a flap template. (See the instructions on page 34.)

⑦ ADD COLORED PAPER FOR CONTRAST

To make your foldnote more interesting, glue contrasting paper to one or both sides of the flap if desired. First, apply glue to the flap. You can protect the rest of your note from stray glue if you first lay the straight edge of a piece of scrap paper down at the fold of the flap.

Next, using a contrasting paper strip that is slightly larger than the flap, lay the straight edge of the strip along the flap's fold and glue it down.

⑧ TRIM THE DECORATIVE PAPER

Trim off the excess contrasting paper with scissors, following the shape of the original flap.

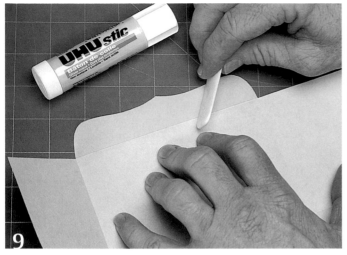

9 BURNISH THE FINISHED FLAP
Burnish and smooth out the completed flap with your bone folder one more time. This will keep the decorative paper from coming unglued.

10 DECORATE THE INSIDE
Decorate the inside of your note with colored pencils, rubber stamps and paper scraps.

Remember that the French Door flaps will keep any cards or photos safe inside, so feel free to add something extra to your correspondence.

11 ADD THE ADDRESS LABELS
Glue torn paper scraps to the outside of your note to make a clean space for writing the addresses. The outer flap can be further accented with a second decorative layer of paper smaller than the first.

TWEEZER TIP
If you are gluing small pieces of paper onto your foldnote, try holding them with a pair of flat-tipped tweezers. They make the job of positioning sticky little scraps much easier, while keeping your fingers clean.

THE CREATIVE ZONE
P.O. BOX 19458
SEATTLE, WASHINGTON
98109-1458

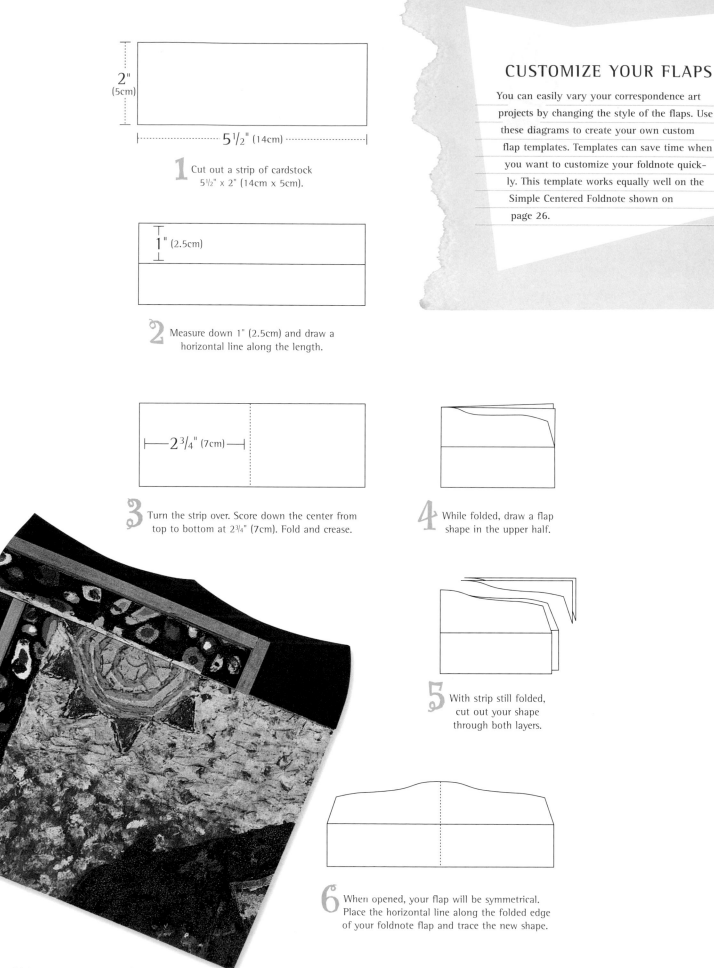

1 Cut out a strip of cardstock 5½" x 2" (14cm x 5cm).

2" (5cm)

5½" (14cm)

1" (2.5cm)

2 Measure down 1" (2.5cm) and draw a horizontal line along the length.

2³/₄" (7cm)

3 Turn the strip over. Score down the center from top to bottom at 2³/₄" (7cm). Fold and crease.

CUSTOMIZE YOUR FLAPS

You can easily vary your correspondence art projects by changing the style of the flaps. Use these diagrams to create your own custom flap templates. Templates can save time when you want to customize your foldnote quickly. This template works equally well on the Simple Centered Foldnote shown on page 26.

4 While folded, draw a flap shape in the upper half.

5 With strip still folded, cut out your shape through both layers.

6 When opened, your flap will be symmetrical. Place the horizontal line along the folded edge of your foldnote flap and trace the new shape.

INTERESTING VariaTions

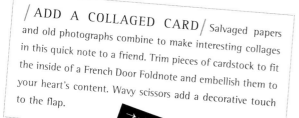

/ ADD A COLLAGED CARD / Salvaged papers and old photographs combine to make interesting collages in this quick note to a friend. Trim pieces of cardstock to fit the inside of a French Door Foldnote and embellish them to your heart's content. Wavy scissors add a decorative touch to the flap.

/ FUN WITH WINDOWS / Give your readers a surprise peek at what's inside. A window or door cut into the flaps of your foldnote adds a visual focal point.

/ ADDRESS LABELS WITH A HEART / Cut heart-shaped masks and place them over the address areas. Then stamp around the edges to turn a plain foldnote into a special greeting.

PocketSurprises

In this chapter we'll introduce you to the Perfect Pocket Foldnote. The element of surprise makes this foldnote as fun to give as it is to receive. What arrives looking like a simple envelope, unfolds to show two pockets just waiting to reveal their hidden secrets. The challenge for you, the sender, is deciding how to tailor your foldnote to that special someone, and what to hide in those two little pockets.

We'll show you how to make four different pocket inserts—from mini pages and paper wreaths to stapled booklets—all from one little pattern. But really, the sky's the limit here. You can stick just about anything into one of these foldnotes. Think about sending lottery tickets for an extra birthday boost. Got some theater tickets you can't use? Send them across town tucked away in a pocket foldnote. Coupons, a clipped article, paper holiday decorations and jokes all make wonderful pocket surprises for those special occasions—or for any time at all.

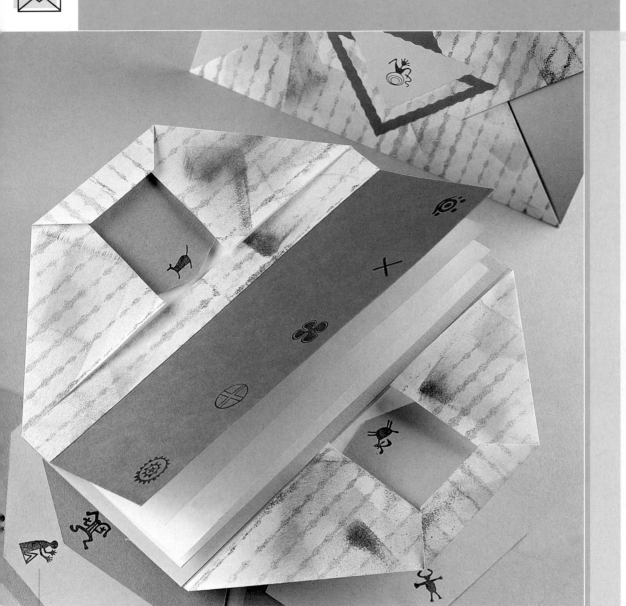

- **foldnote:** 8½" x 11" (21.6cm x 28cm) sheet of decorative paper (GRAIN SHORT)

- **pages:** two sheets of 8½" x 11" (21.6cm x 28cm) colored text-weight paper

- 8½" x 11" (21.6cm x 28cm) sheet of colored cardstock

- ruler

- pencil

- bone folder

- pocket insert pattern (ON PAGE 39)

- scissors or craft knife

- cutting mat

- glue stick

- decorative paper scraps

- rubber stamps

- black ink pad

The element of surprise makes this foldnote especially fun to send and receive. Unfold the note to discover hidden pockets just waiting to share their secrets. Perfect receptacles for mini pages or booklets (see the insert ideas on pages 43–47), these pockets might also hold tickets or coupons for that special someone's special day.

Perfect Pocket Foldnote

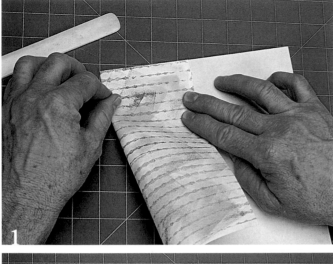

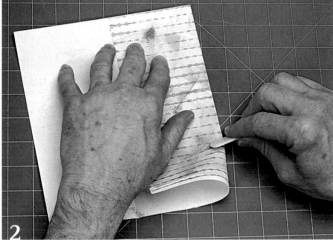

1 MEASURE AND FOLD
THE LEFT EDGE OF THE PAPER

Place the foldnote paper horizontally on your work surface, decorative side down. Starting from the left edge, measure over and make pencil marks at 4" (10.2cm) and 7" (17.8cm) close to the top edge. Fold the left edge of the paper to the 7" (17.8cm) mark, aligning the top edges. Crease the fold with a bone folder and open it up.

2 FOLD THE RIGHT
EDGE OF THE PAPER

Fold the right edge of the paper to the 4" (10.2cm) mark, align the top edges, then crease and open.

This is the pattern for custom pages you can tuck into your pocket foldnote. To use this template, copy it at 100% onto a piece of cardstock and cut it out.

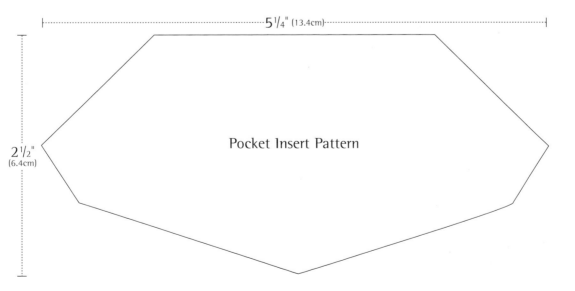

5¹⁄₄" (13.4cm)

2¹⁄₂" (6.4cm)

Pocket Insert Pattern

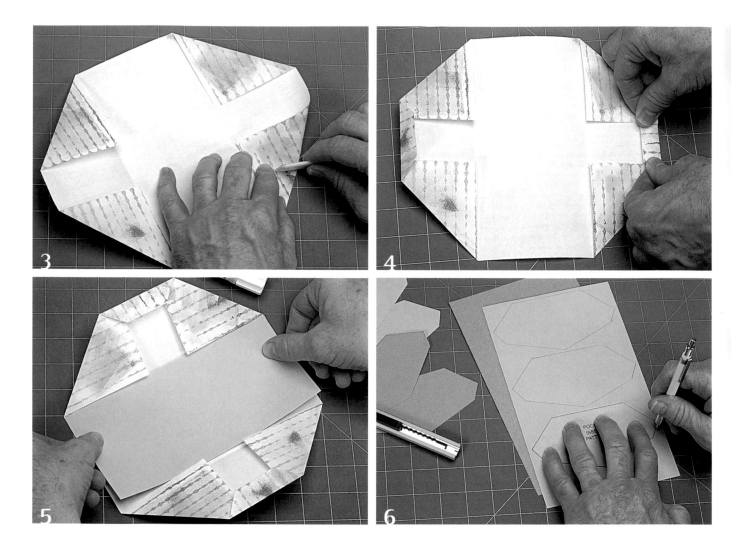

3 FOLD THE CORNERS

Fold each corner in to the nearest fold line and crease them with a bone folder.

4 FOLD IN FLAPS ON BOTH SIDES

With your foldnote still in a horizontal position, make pencil marks 1½" (3.8cm) in from each side. Fold both sides in to the pencil marks, creating ¾" (1.9cm) flaps and crease them well.

5 GLUE CARDSTOCK INTO THE CENTER SECTION

Cut a strip of cardstock 8½" (21.6cm) x 3⅞" (9.8cm) and glue it to the center section of the foldnote for stiffness and color contrast.

6 TRACE YOUR NOTE PAGES

Photocopy the pocket insert pattern on page 39 to a piece of cardstock and cut out carefully. This pattern will be used for each pocket insert. Trace your pattern on colored paper for individual note pages.

7 DECORATE YOUR PAGES WITH STAMPS
Decorate your pocket note pages. When you're done writing your letter, tuck the pages snugly inside the pockets.

8 ADD A STICKER TO THE FLAPS
Close your foldnote and add a handmade sticker to seal the flap.

9 THE FINISHED POCKET FOLDNOTE
The side pockets can hold any number of surprises. Jot down a short poem, or send a series of humorous pictures.

TAKE IT A STEP FURTHER NEED MORE SPACE FOR WRITING? ADD A STAPLED BOOKLET INSERT TO YOUR POCKET FOLD- NOTE BY FOLLOWING THE INSTRUCTIONS ON PAGE 42. →

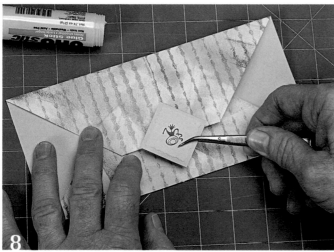

CREATIVE INSERTS

Add some further excitement by using your pocket insert pattern for more than just making loose pages. Go wild with one of the four different pocket insert variations found on pages 43–47.

STAPLED BOOKLET INSERT

The beauty of the Pocket Foldnote is that there's plenty of room to play around with enclosure variations. When you have lots to say, make a stapled booklet and glue it to the middle section of your foldnote for added writing space. Make your covers from two pieces of cardstock cut to 8½" x 3⅞" (21.6cm x 9.8cm) grain long. Choose a light-colored text-weight paper and cut four inside pages to 8" x 3⅝" (20.3cm x 9.2cm). Trim a scrap of decorative paper to 1½" x 8½" (3.8cm x 21.6cm) to wrap around the booklet spine.

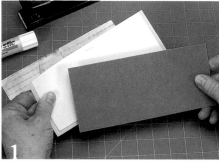

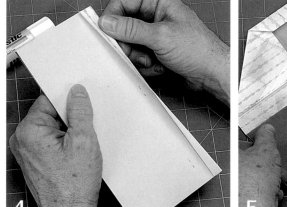

❶ STAPLE THE INSIDE PAGES
Square up your pages, then put one staple in the middle of the spine area, close to the top edge, to hold the pages together. Center your pages inside the covers, flush with the top edge.

❷ ATTACH THE COVERS
Place three staples along the spine, ¾" (1.9cm) from the top edge. Gently flatten the staples by tapping with a small hammer or the blunt end of a round-handled craft knife.

❸ SCORE THE COVER FLAP
Measure down 1" (2.5cm) from the edge of the spine and score your top cover. Fold and crease. This will make it easier to open your booklet.

❹ ADD A DECORATIVE STRIP
Glue up the inside surface of your decorative paper strip. Starting at the score line on the front cover, adhere the paper and wrap it around the spine to the back cover as shown. Burnish the spine well.

❺ INSERT THE BOOKLET INTO YOUR FOLDNOTE
Glue the back surface of your booklet and adhere it to the middle section of your Pocket Foldnote. We've added stamped images from Ivory Coast.

POCKET INSERTS

One little pattern, so many creative combinations! The next four inserts are all made from the basic pocket insert pattern on page 39, but depending on how you fold your paper, where you place the pattern, or what you do with the pages, each one lends new meaning to "variety is the spice of correspondence art." Instructions for each one begin on page 44.

stapled POCKET INSERT

A few staples and decorative paper scraps will turn loose pages into mini-booklets. Send separate letters to your niece and nephew in the same foldnote; or write your letter in one and a teeny weeny story in the other. Our booklets have four pages, but there's certainly room for more. (See page 44.)

folded POCKET INSERT

For this insert, tracing the pattern to a folded piece of paper creates a whole different animal, so to speak. Colored pages can be trimmed and nested inside one another to create layered letters as fun to look at as they are to read. (See page 45.)

wreath POCKET INSERT

There's something very inviting about a circular wreath. Our Wreath Insert can definitely be decked out for the holidays, or delight your friends and family at any time of the year. (See page 46.)

accordion POCKET INSERT

Accordion folds are among the most popular folds, perhaps because they're so versatile and dramatic. You start with something that is one size and when you open it, end up with so much more. (See page 47.)

stapled POCKET INSERT

For each stapled pocket insert you will need colored cardstock for the covers, colored text-weight paper for the inside pages and decorative paper to wrap around the spine. These booklets have four pages, but there's always room for more.

❶ TRACE THE PAGES AND COVERS
Trace the pocket insert pattern from page 39 eight times on contrasting colored paper for your pages and four times on cardstock for your covers. When tracing the pattern, be sure to have the longest (top) edge of the pattern parallel to the grain of the paper or cardstock.

Cut out your pages and covers. Next, measure and score the top covers with a bone folder ½" (1.3cm) from the long straight edge.

❷ STAPLE THE PAGES
Place four pages between two covers and staple twice in the middle of the spine area. Repeat for your second booklet, then flatten all the staples.

❸ ADD A DECORATIVE SPINE WRAP
Fold both pieces of decorative paper in half along the length, decorative side out, and crease. Glue up the inside surface of one and slip it over the spine of one booklet to cover the staples. Make sure the wrap is snug, then burnish it on both sides with your bone folder. Repeat these steps for the second booklet.

❹ ADD THE FINAL TOUCHES
Trim the ends of your wraps flush with the angled edges of the inserts.

Make a coordinating Pocket Foldnote, and tie everything together with matching spine wraps and cardstock for a truly sophisticated mail-art package.

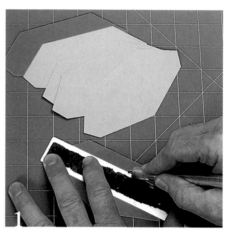

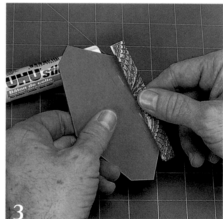

folded POCKET INSERT

Nest different colored pages inside one another for a dramatic layered effect. This insert is easy to make and fun to embellish. For these pages you will need four colored text-weight papers each cut to 5¼" (13.3cm) square.

❶ FOLD EACH SQUARE
Fold your colored squares in half with the fold parallel to the grain and crease with a bone folder.

❷ TRACE THE PATTERN
Place one folded square inside another, then trace the pattern from page 39 with the longest straight edge on the fold. Repeat these steps for the remaining squares.

❸ CUT OUT THE SHAPES
With the pages still folded and nested, cut out the traced shapes. Trim the edges of your outer covers with decorative scissors if desired, to expose the colored edges of your inner pages.

❹ DECORATE THE COVERS
Decorate the outer covers with simple geometric paper shapes.

❺ ADD FURTHER EMBELLISHMENTS
There are numerous ways to add flair to your foldnotes. Here, we've added a deckled edge to the black cardstock in the center, which ties it visually to the inserts. It's subtle, but effective.

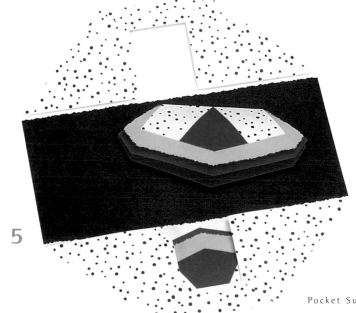

wreath POCKET INSERT

With a wreath, you can write your letter in each folded section, or in a circle around and around the center. For each wreath you make, you will need a sheet of colored text-weight paper cut to 8½" (21.6cm) square.

❶ FOLD ON THE DIAGONAL
Fold one square in half diagonally and crease the fold with a bone folder.

❷ FOLD IN HALF AGAIN
Fold it in half again, bringing the points at either end of the folded edge together and crease.

❸ TRACE THE PATTERN
Place your folded triangle with the open edges facing you, then trace the pattern from page 39 as shown.

❹ CUT OUT THE WREATH
Remove the pattern and cut the traced lines through all layers. Repeat these steps for your second wreath.

❺ DECORATE THE WREATH PAGES
We've used our foldnote paper again to frame the wreath opening and to add decorative touches around the outer edge. Consider stamping or writing on the inside of the pocket.

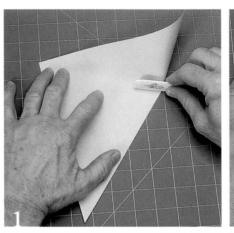

accordion POCKET INSERT

For this project, make the same insert look totally different just by combining your papers in different ways. You will need a 5½" x 9½" (14cm x 24.1cm) piece of colored text-weight paper (grain short) for each insert.

❶ FOLD PAPER IN HALF
Place your paper horizontally. Fold one side over to the other and crease well with a bone folder. Open the paper and flip it over.

❷ MARK AND FOLD OVER THE EDGES
Measuring from the left edge, make pencil marks at 4" (10.2cm) and 5½" (14cm) close to the top edge.

Fold the left edge over to the 5½" (14cm) mark, aligning the top and bottom edges, then crease and open. Fold the right edge over to the 4" (10.2cm) mark, align the edges, crease and open.

❸ ACCORDION FOLD THE PAPER
Accordion fold the paper. Notice that the center fold is recessed—that's intentional. Place the longest edge of the pattern from page 39 on the folds and trace.

❹ CUT OUT THE PATTERN
Cut out the pattern shape through all the layers. Repeat these steps for the second piece of paper. Then decorate each accordion insert with colorful scraps of paper.

❺ COORDINATE THE PAGES AND THE FOLDNOTE
Decorative edge cutters are a nice optional tool when working with paper. Here, the small wavy edges on the decorative papers add contrast to the straight edges on the rest of the foldnote.

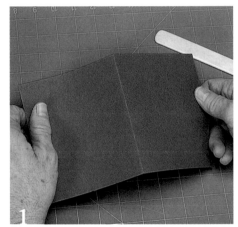

MoreFunWithFolds

So much to do, so little time. Real or imagined, time does seem to be speeding us faster and faster. Yet, nieces and nephews still have birthdays, friends still invite us to special events, life still keeps happening, whether we have time for it or not. So what do you do when time is of the essence and you need to send a thank you? Or you want to say "Hey, howdy!" to your sister and an e-mail just won't cut it? We say, make more foldnotes!

Foldnotes are so quick and easy that a lack of time is really not an issue. Simply make a few folds in a piece of paper and you have the note and envelope all in one. Want more substance? Add a creative insert. Or photos. Or see-through address windows. The following projects show you how. And in the making, we hope you discover the best reason of all for sending foldnotes—they're just plain fun! Really, in these times of hurry, hurry, hurry, couldn't we all use just a little more fun?

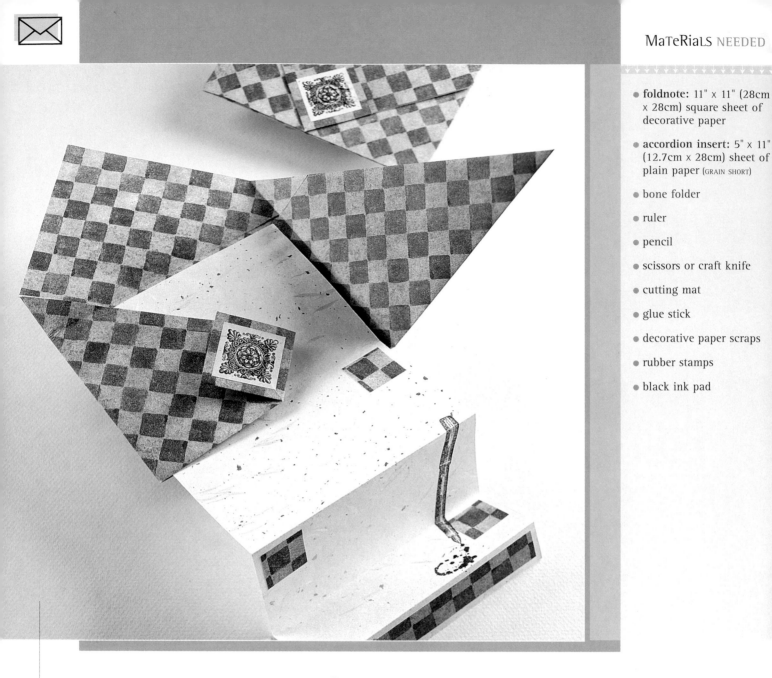

- **foldnote:** 11" x 11" (28cm x 28cm) square sheet of decorative paper

- **accordion insert:** 5" x 11" (12.7cm x 28cm) sheet of plain paper (GRAIN SHORT)

- bone folder

- ruler

- pencil

- scissors or craft knife

- cutting mat

- glue stick

- decorative paper scraps

- rubber stamps

- black ink pad

Of all the projects in this book, the Diamond Foldnote is like the "hostess with the mostest" who always has room for one more at the table. Made from the largest piece of paper, the finished note offers the most writing surface and plenty of opportunity to add even more writing surface and more surprises. Like its name, this one is a true gem.

Diamond Foldnote

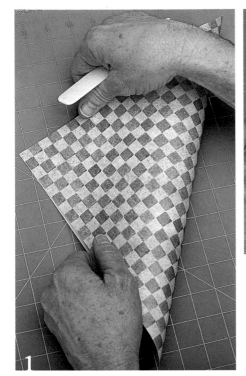

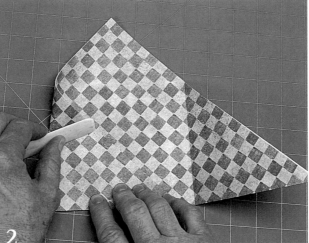

1 FOLD THE SQUARE ON THE DIAGONAL

Fold an 11" x 11" (28cm x 28cm) square in half diagonally and crease the fold well with a bone folder.

2 MEASURE AND FOLD THE SIDE FLAPS

Place your ruler along the folded edge. Measuring from the left, make pencil marks at 5½" (14cm) and 10" (25.4cm). Fold the right point over to the left pencil mark and crease heavily, then unfold. Now fold the left point over to the right mark, crease heavily and unfold. Erase your pencil marks.

3 FOLD BACK THE TIP OF THE LEFT FLAP

Fold both points over again with the left point on top. Then take the tip of the left point and fold it back to the left so that the new vertical fold is at the bottom of the V formed by the overlapping sections of the foldnote. Crease this fold hard with your bone folder.

4 OPEN UP THE DIAMOND POCKET

Take the left point and raise it to a standing position. Holding both sides of the point open between your thumbs and forefingers, push the point forward to create a diamond pocket. Crease the folds with your bone folder.

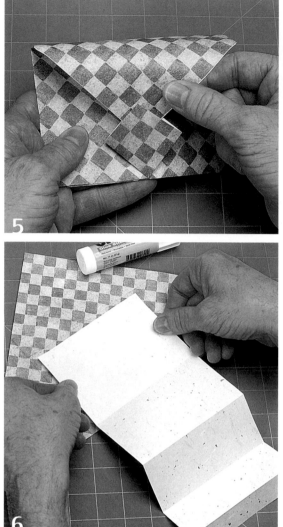

⑤ TUCK THE TOP FLAP INTO THE POCKET

Fold the remaining top point of the foldnote down to the bottom center of your foldnote and crease heavily. Now lift the top flap and stick the point into the diamond pocket. Your Diamond Foldnote is ready to decorate.

⑥ ADD AN ACCORDION LETTER

To add more writing surface inside, lay your plain paper in the center rectangle of the triangle and begin accordion pleating. No measuring is necessary—the sections of your accordion letter can be different sizes as long as it all fits inside the foldnote. Then run your glue stick along the top edge on the back side of the accordion letter and glue it into the rectangle.

⑦ ADD THE FINAL TOUCHES

In our foldnote, the panels of the accordion get smaller and smaller. We use the last panel as the hand-pull that opens the letter. A few rubber stamps and pasted scraps of decorative paper complete the elegant look of this design.

TAKE IT A STEP FURTHER TRIANGLE POP-OUTS ARE A CLEVER WAY TO ADD SOME DIMENSION TO YOUR DIAMOND FOLDNOTE. ADD A FEW TO YOUR FOLDNOTE BY FOLLOWING THE INSTRUCTIONS ON THE NEXT PAGE. →

WRITING SPACE OPTIONS

Your letter can be written on the accordion letter pasted into the Diamond Foldnote, or you can open up the entire inside surface of the foldnote and write on the additional blank space inside—an unexpected surprise.

triangle POP-OUT INSERT

With all that writing surface inside the Diamond Foldnote, we still can't resist adding more. This simple triangular pop-out can be positioned anywhere inside your fold-note to create a truly surprising piece of interactive mail. For each pop-out you will need a 5" x 5" (12.7cm x 12.7cm) square piece of colored text-weight paper.

❶ FOLD A SQUARE ON THE DIAGONALS
Fold a 5" (12.7cm) square diagonally, crease and unfold. Now fold it diagonally the other way on the same side of the paper. Your diagonal folds should intersect in the middle.

❷ FLIP THE SQUARE OVER AND FOLD IN HALF
Turn your square over. Fold it once in half, bringing the bottom edge of the square up to the top edge. Crease well and unfold.

❸ PUSH IN THE CENTER
Turn your square over again and with one finger, push down at the center. The ends of the horizontal fold should pop up.

❹ BRING IN THE ENDS TO MAKE A TRIANGLE
Bring the opposite ends of the horizontal fold together, then lay it down and flatten your triangle. Crease the folds well. Your pop-out is ready to be added to your foldnote.

❺ DECORATE AND GLUE IN YOUR POP-OUTS
Once you've finished making your pop-outs, decorate and write on them, then glue them into any available section of your Diamond Foldnote. If you wish, you can even open up the entire inside of your foldnote and paste a few pop-outs in there as well!

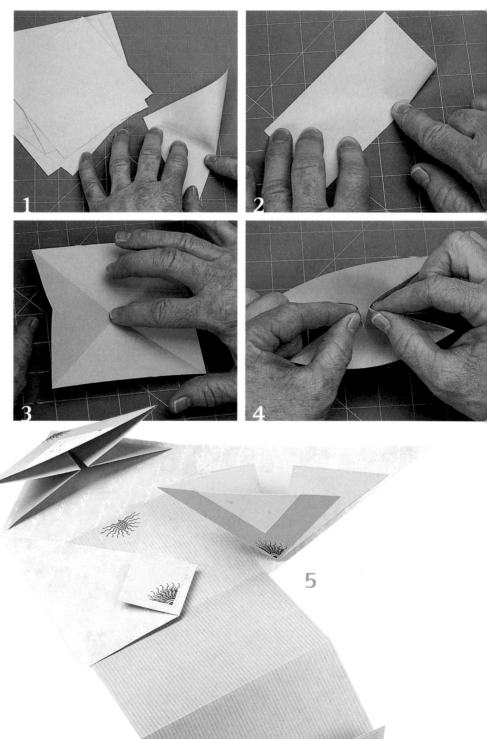

- **foldnote**: 8½" x 8½" (21.6cm x 21.6cm) square sheet of decorative paper

- **insert**: 11" x 4⅛" (28cm x 10.5cm) piece of cardstock (GRAIN SHORT)

- ruler

- pencil

- bone folder

- glue stick

- decorative paper scraps

- rubber stamps

- black ink pad

- oval template for insert

- photos or images for insert

The Square Foldnote is one of our most practical. Quickly made, it easily adapts to handle different enclosures—like the French Door insert we include for you here. Dress it up or leave it plain, write on the inside surface, cut individual pages for your letter, or include a special address window on the outside (see page 57). There's no end to this note's versatility.

Easy Square Foldnote

1 MARK THE DIAGONALS

Place your paper decorative side down and draw two light diagonal pencil lines that intersect in the center of your paper. Place the paper in front of you so the pencil lines run north/south and east/west. Make two pencil marks on the horizontal (E/W) line 1¾" (4.5cm) to the left and 1¾" (4.5cm) to the right of the center point.

2 FOLD IN THE TOP AND BOTTOM

Fold the north and south points in to the center and crease them with your bone folder.

3 FOLD IN THE REMAINING POINTS

Turn your paper so the remaining points are north and south. Fold the top point down to the bottom pencil dot, crease and open. Fold the bottom point up to the top pencil dot, crease it and leave it folded.

4 FOLD THE TOP FLAP DOWN

To finish the foldnote, fold the top point down approximately 1 to 1½" (2.5cm to 4.5cm) and make a second crease. Now fold the entire top flap down. Your foldnote is complete and ready for contents and decorative touches.

5 CREATE A FRENCH DOOR INSERT

Place an 11" x 4⅛" (28cm x 10.5cm) piece of cardstock horizontally, plain side up. For smoother folds, cut this cardstock with the grain running parallel to the short edge of the paper.

Measure from the left and make pencil marks at the top and bottom, at 2⅝" (6.7cm) and 8⅜" (21.3cm). Align your ruler with each set of marks and make a valley score. Fold and crease each line.

6 ADD PICTURE WINDOWS
TO EACH PANEL
Trace appropriate-sized ovals on one or
both door panels, then cut out the shapes.

7 INSERT YOUR PHOTOS
Glue or tape your photos or images
behind the window openings. If
you're using double-stick tape,
place all the pieces before peeling
off the top protective paper. Then
attach the photo.

8 COVER THE PHOTO BACKS
WITH DECORATIVE PAPER
Line each window panel with paper
to cover the back of the photo and
give your insert a finished look.

9 DECORATE THE FRENCH DOORS
Add faux photo corners to the front of the
doors for a decorative touch. Here, we've
used different photos of our nephew and
stamped below the words *Now* and *Then*
on decorative paper scraps.

Write a note inside your French Door
insert, tuck it into your Square Foldnote
and send it on its way.

TRY A FUN VARIATION ADD A SEE-THROUGH ADDRESS WIN-
DOW TO YOUR FOLDNOTE BY FOLLOWING THE INSTRUCTIONS ON
THE NEXT PAGE. →

ACETATE ADDRESS WINDOWS

We like address windows because they add dimension to correspondence. Put a window on the front of your Square Foldnote and you invite the viewer to "C'mon in and visit with me a spell." Try layering different colored windows for even more dimension. For the acetate windows, you will need one or more contrasting papers and a piece of acetate or polyester film, all 4¼" x 6" (10.8cm x 15.2cm) in size.

① CUT OUT AN ADDRESS WINDOW
Make a Square Foldnote. With your foldnote open, trace a window shape on the center rectangle and cut it out. Leave at least a ¾" (1.9cm) border on all sides. Trim the inside pages and acetate.

② TRACE THE WINDOW
Place a piece of 4¼" x 6" (10.8cm x 15.2cm) colored paper inside your foldnote and close it, then trace the address opening on the inside paper.

③ ADDRESS THE SPACE
Remove the paper and stamp or write the address within the drawn shape. If you plan to add another layer, leave some space between the address and the traced opening.

④ ADD A CONTRASTING FRAME
To create a layered frame, trace the original opening on a different colored paper, then cut out a slightly smaller opening.

⑤ ASSEMBLE THE LAYERS
To send, place the acetate window in first, then the address paper. You may find it easier to cut out and layer your windows, then stamp your address in the space left over. You can also save time by making cardstock templates, so all you have to do is trace the different-sized openings on future foldnotes.

5

- **foldnote:** 8½" x 11"
  (21.6cm x 28cm) sheet
  of decorative paper

- ruler

- bone folder

- glue stick

- decorative paper scraps

- rubber stamps

- black ink pad

- postage stamp

The story we've been told over the years is that the Mennonites designed this foldnote to eliminate the cost of an envelope. While their motives may have been thrifty, the resulting foldnote is worth its weight in gold. Simple, clever and beautiful, it requires no measuring or cutting, and we especially like the way the postage stamp does extra duty as the sticker that seals the note.

Mennonite Foldnote

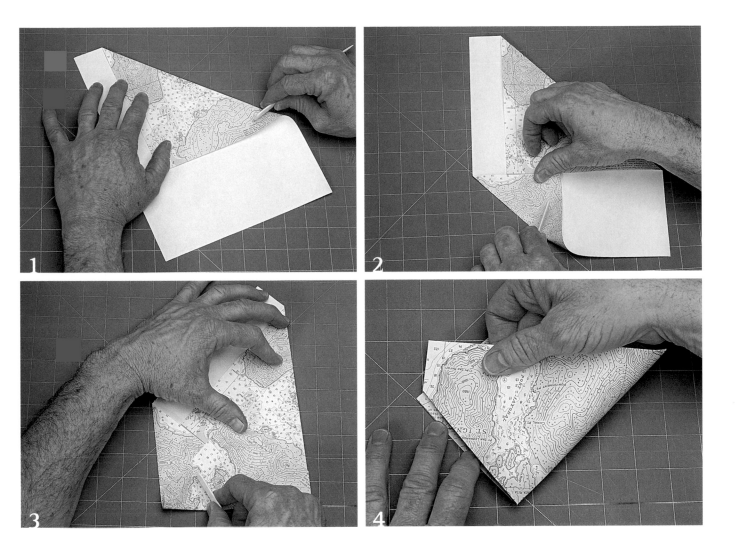

1 FOLD THE TOP-RIGHT CORNER DOWN

With your paper placed vertically and decorated side down, fold the top-right corner down leaving approximately a 1½" (3.8cm) margin on the left side. Make sure your edges are parallel, then crease the fold with your bone folder.

2 FOLD THE BOTTOM-LEFT CORNER UP

Fold the bottom-left corner up to meet the edge of the first folded corner and crease.

3 TURN THE NOTE AND FOLD THE BOTTOM CORNER UP

Turn your note slightly so that the bottom-right corner now points south. Fold the bottom corner up approximately 4" (10.2cm), keeping the side edges parallel, and crease the fold.

4 FOLD LAST CORNER UP OVER TOP EDGE

Swing the note around 180 degrees so the remaining corner now points south. Fold this last corner up so the top part of the point is sticking above the top edge of your foldnote and crease.

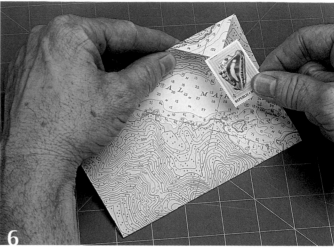

5 FLIP THE NOTE OVER AND FOLD THE TIP DOWN
Flip the note over and fold the little triangle down.
Unfold your note and you're ready to decorate.

6 WRITE YOUR LETTER
AND SEAL WITH A STAMP
You can write directly on the foldnote, or create individual stationery
pages. When you're done writing
your letter, close it up, fold the last
little triangle down and seal the
foldnote with your postage stamp.

We show a decorative foreign
stamp here, but of course you will
want to use correct postage to mail
your Mennonite Foldnote.

7 DECORATE THE FOLDNOTE
Finish by cutting paper into
organic shapes to create address
labels that mimic the shapes
found on the nautical map.

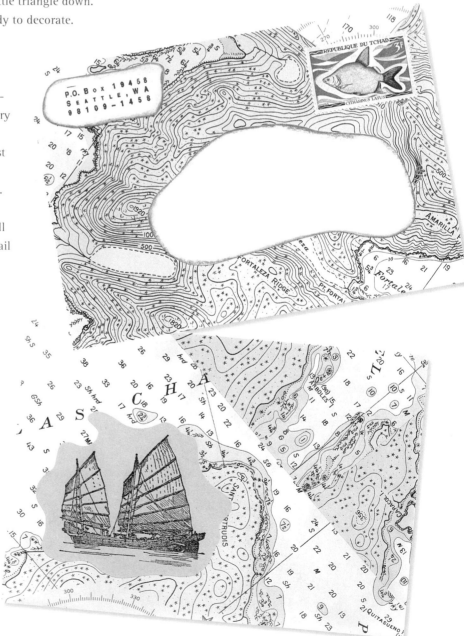

/ DROP IN A BOOKLET / Instead of loose pages, why not put in a booklet with French Door flaps? We adjusted the sides of this Square Foldnote to make a wider foldnote. Then we created a booklet just the right size to drop inside.

Take Time to Play
It is the secret
of youth and stability

/ ELEGANT DIAMONDS / A hand-carved stamp lends a touch of oriental elegance to this Diamond Foldnote. Inside, yellow pop-outs provide a brilliant contrast to the red and black exterior.

/ MORE FUN WITH WINDOWS /
Acetate windows can be used for more than just addresses. They also make perfect frames for a piece of art or a holiday greeting.

M≠J
POB 19458
SEATTLE
WA 98109

OH YES!

MagicUpYourSleeves

Like a magician making objects appear and disappear, these cardstock mail-art sleeves will surprise and delight your audience with the paper magic they perform. Versatile and venerable in their simplicity, they make the perfect foil for creative combinations of inserts and embellishments—mix and match your favorite inserts or decorating ideas from any other project with a sleeve and see what happens. And because sleeves are so accommodating, they can be transformed quick as a wink to a different size simply by slicing off one end.

In this chapter, we conjure up the basic sleeve from a single piece of cardstock that has been decorated with food coloring and blown bubbles, then show you how to add decorative flaps to keep your creative contents from doing a disappearing act. We follow that with four multitalented inserts: an accordion letter, a shopping bag letter that doubles as art, and two variations of a photo frame letter. Start sending out correspondence magic like this and you'll have everyone begging for more.

- **sleeve:** 8½" x 11" (21.6cm x 29.2cm) sheet of card-stock (GRAIN SHORT)
- ruler
- pencil
- bone folder
- scissors or craft knife
- cutting mat
- decorative cutter (OPTIONAL)
- hole punch
- glue stick
- decorative paper scraps

Think of the sleeve as the workhorse of mail art. Made from cardstock, a sleeve provides a sturdy platform from which to launch interactive letters that run the gamut from simple to complex, funky to trés elegant. Choose cardstock from a wonderful variety of colors and designs, or decorate your own as you see here.

Basic Correspondence Sleeve

1 MEASURE AND MARK YOUR FOLDS

Place your large cardstock horizontally with the decorated side down. Measuring from the left, make pencil marks at the top and bottom at 2¼" (5.7cm) and 6¾" (17.2cm).

2 SCORE YOUR FOLDS

Score with a bone folder or scoring tool, fold the cardstock and crease at the pencil marks.

3 ADD A SEAL

Glue a colorful handmade seal to the top flap to complete your sleeve.

TAKE IT A STEP FURTHER YOUR BASIC SLEEVE IS NOW READY TO BE FILLED. IF YOU PLAN TO INSERT LOOSE PAGES, TURN THE PAGE TO LEARN HOW TO ADD DECORATIVE SIDE FLAPS.

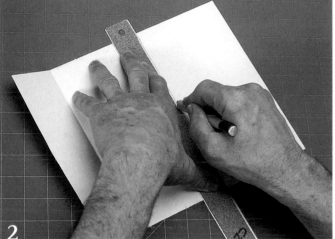

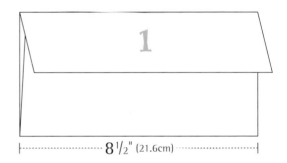

8½" (21.6cm)

7½" (19.1cm)

SLEEVES OF ALL SIZES

The basic sleeve is made from 8½" x 11" (21.6cm x 28cm) cardstock. Score and fold according to the directions above, then trim one end to vary the width. You can make custom sleeves by varying the width and height. All three of the widths shown here meet standard U.S. postal regulations.

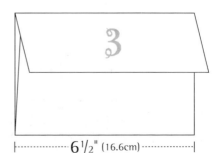

6½" (16.6cm)

ADDING FLAPS TO A BASIC SLEEVE

Adding flaps is a great way to dress up a basic correspondence sleeve. Better yet, flaps will keep any note pages or other enclosures from falling out. To create flaps for this sleeve you will need a 4¾" x 11" (12.1cm x 28cm) piece of cardstock (grain short) and some decorative paper scraps.

1 MEASURE AND MARK YOUR FLAPS
With your 4¾" x 11" (12.1cm x 28cm) piece of cardstock placed horizontally, measure from the left and make pencil marks at the top and bottom at 1¼" (3.2cm), 5½" (14cm) and 9¾" (24.8cm).

2 SCORE AND FOLD THE FLAPS
Align your ruler with each outer set of marks. With your scoring tool, valley score and crease these two outer lines.

3 CUT THE FLAPS APART AND SHAPE THEM
Cut the flaps apart at the middle line, then shape your flaps at either or both ends if desired. We've used straight lines coming to a point, but you could round the ends or cut them with a decorative cutter.

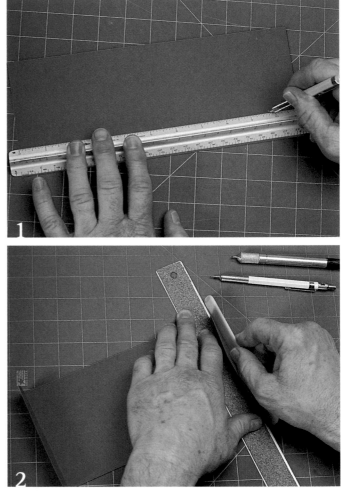

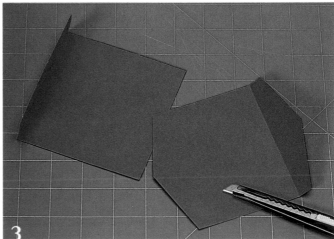

FOLDING PERFECT FLAPS

How can you make your flaps fold easily and lie flat? Cut this piece of cardstock grain short, with the paper grain running parallel to the short edge of the cardstock. (See page 15 for more on grain direction.)

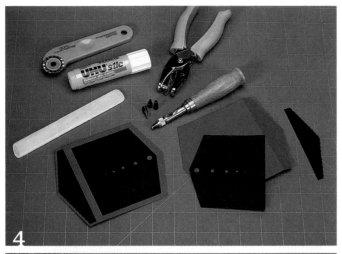

4 DECORATE THE FLAPS

It's much easier to decorate your flaps before you attach them to the sleeve. Try cutting out contrasting paper that mimics the shape of the flap, then add wavy edges and punched holes for visual interest.

5 ATTACH THE FLAPS TO THE BASIC SLEEVE

Flaps can be glued to the inside or the outside of a sleeve. We're gluing the short section of our flaps to the outside surface of the sleeve so that the large sections wrap around to the inside.

6 ADD MATCHING STATIONERY

Our sleeve with flaps holds stationery with crayon rubbings of found objects. Notice how the flap sections glued to the outside become a design element for the address surface.

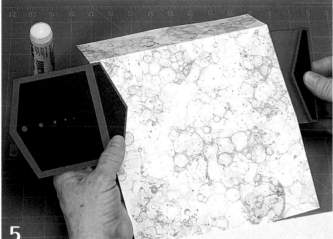

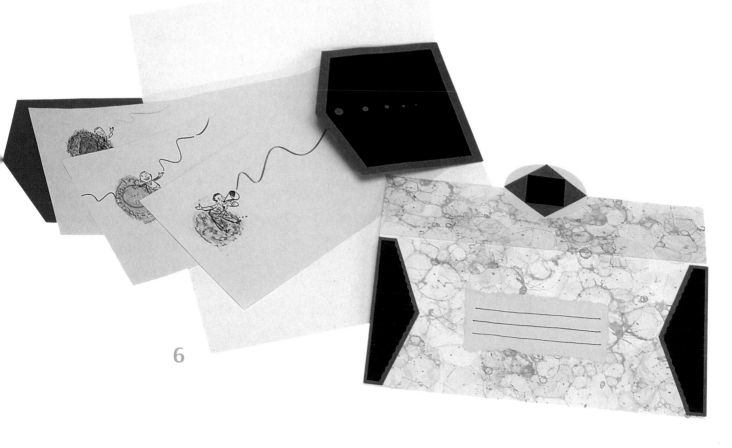

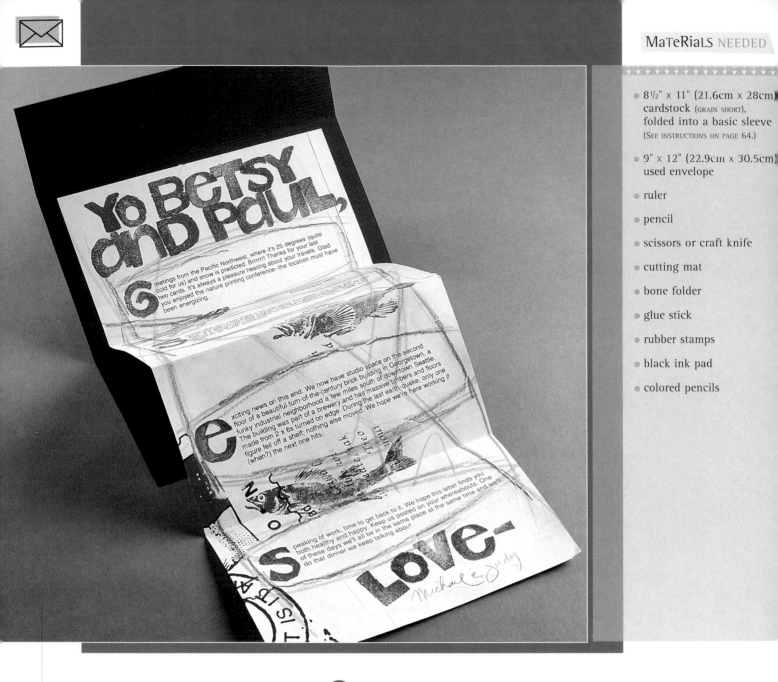

- 8½" x 11" (21.6cm x 28cm) cardstock (GRAIN SHORT), folded into a basic sleeve (SEE INSTRUCTIONS ON PAGE 64.)

- 9" x 12" (22.9cm x 30.5cm) used envelope

- ruler

- pencil

- scissors or craft knife

- cutting mat

- bone folder

- glue stick

- rubber stamps

- black ink pad

- colored pencils

Envelopes are one of our favorite sources of earth-friendly stationery, which is why you see a lot of them in our projects. Here's a simple way to reuse a large envelope. Open one up and you have a piece of paper approximately 24" (61cm) long, perfect for the accordion fold and more exciting than plain paper, especially if you include the outside printing and postage in your letter.

Recycled Envelope Insert

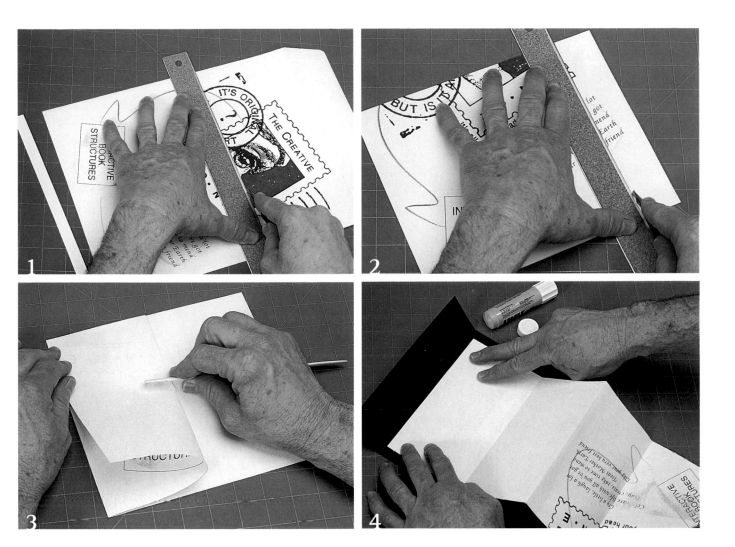

1 CUT OFF THE TOP AND BOTTOM

Choose a large, colorful envelope, at least 9" x 12" (22.9cm x 30.5cm). Place it horizontally, with the bottom of the envelope facing left. Measure from the left and draw vertical lines at ½" (1.3cm) and 8" (20.3cm). Cut through both layers of paper on these lines.

2 CUT OFF ONE FOLDED EDGE

Turn what's left of your envelope so the folded edges are on the sides. Measuring from the left, make pencil marks at the top and bottom at 8" (20.3cm). Align your ruler with these marks and cut through both layers of paper on this line.

3 FOLD THE PAPER LIKE AN ACCORDION

Leaving your paper in the same position, fold the top cut edge on the right over to the folded edge on the left and crease. Then flip your paper over and fold the remaining cut edge back to the fold and crease.

4 ATTACH IT TO A BASIC SLEEVE AND WRITE YOUR LETTER

Apply glue to the back of the top panel and adhere it to the middle section of your sleeve. Then, embellish and write your letter. Our letter was printed from the computer, then torn apart and pasted onto the accordion panels. The large letters were stamped with Michael's 37-year-old hand-carved eraser set, then the letters were colored in with pencil.

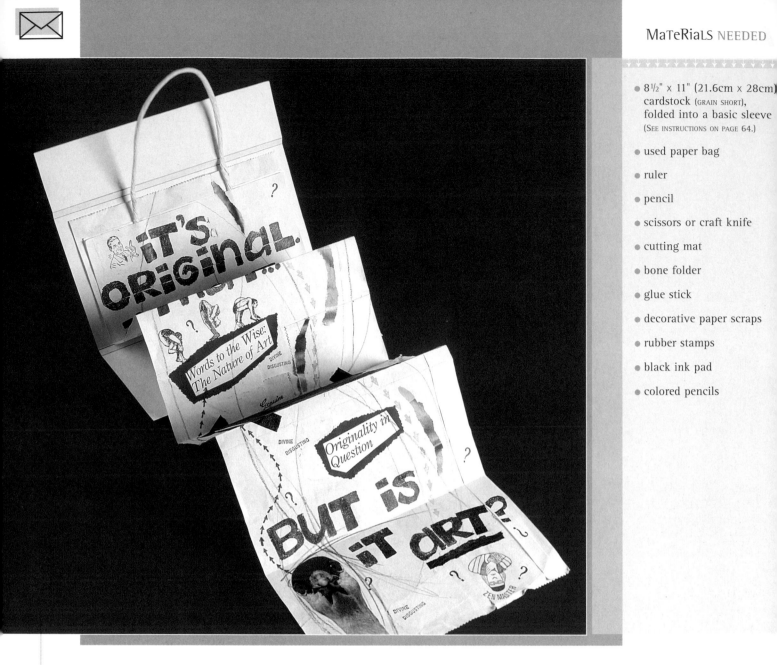

- 8½" x 11" (21.6cm x 28cm) cardstock (GRAIN SHORT), folded into a basic sleeve (SEE INSTRUCTIONS ON PAGE 64.)

- used paper bag

- ruler

- pencil

- scissors or craft knife

- cutting mat

- bone folder

- glue stick

- decorative paper scraps

- rubber stamps

- black ink pad

- colored pencils

Whoever invented shopping bags with handles gets our vote of thanks. When slit down the sides and opened up, a paper bag is the perfect canvas for correspondence art. Write on the clean inside of the bag, or incorporate the outer bag design into your letter. And the really fun part? The handle acts as a hanger, just in case your letter ends up on the wall. And you thought shopping bags were just for shopping!

Letter In a Bag

1 TRIM YOUR BAG

You will be inserting this bag into a basic sleeve (see page 64), so trim off both sides of the bag to fit the width of your sleeve. Open the bag up and cut off the handle at the bottom.

2 FOLD THE BAG TO FIT THE SLEEVE

Place the top edge of the bag in the middle section of your sleeve. Pleat the bag back and forth accordion style so that the sections are about 4¼" (10.8cm) high. Continue pleating until you run out of bag.

3 WRITE YOUR MASTERPIECE

Now comes the fun part: create your paper bag masterpiece. Ours has everything but the kitchen sink—hand-carved letters, clip art images, word stamps, collage and colored pencil.

4 ADJUST THE OUTER SLEEVE

Because this letter tends to be thick, your sleeve must be adjusted to accommodate it. To do this, measure over ¼" (6mm) to the outside of each existing fold and mark these lines. Score and crease these two additional folds.

5 GLUE IN THE PAPER BAG

Glue the back surface of your handle section to the inside center of the sleeve and burnish. When folded up, the sleeve now has the capacity to hold the paper bag and whatever you add to it.

6 ADD THE FINAL TOUCHES

Notice here how the back of the bottom panel of our letter ends up on top when the accordion is folded up—providing one more surface to decorate.

- 8½" x 11" (21.6cm x 28cm) cardstock (GRAIN SHORT), folded into a basic sleeve (SEE INSTRUCTIONS ON PAGE 64.)

- frame insert: 8½" x 11" (21.6cm x 28cm) colored cardstock

- bone folder

- ruler

- pencil

- scissors and craft knife

- cutting mat

- oval template

- glue stick or double-stick tape

- photos

- rubber stamps

- black ink pad

- decorative paper scraps

- decorative scissors

DEAR GRANDMA,

Our families spend a lot of time both behind and in front of the camera, so we enjoy finding ways to showcase photos for mail travel. This picture-perfect project requires only two folds and a little cutting to create a frame letter that holds one or two photos, and can be shaped and decorated to fit your fancy.

Doubletake Photo Flaps

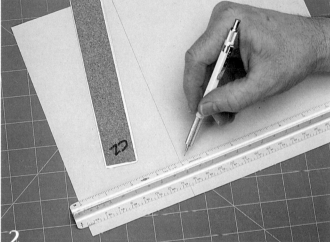

1 FOLD THE CARDSTOCK
IN HALF LENGTHWISE

Place your 8½" x 11" (21.6cm x 28cm) cardstock for the insert vertically on your work surface. Measure from the left and make pencil marks top and bottom at 4¼" (10.8cm). Score and fold your cardstock in half lengthwise. Crease well with a bone folder.

2 DRAW A LINE PERPENDICULAR
TO THE FOLD

Open up your cardstock and place it horizontally on your work surface, decorated side down. Measuring from the left edge, make pencil marks at the top and bottom at 4" (10.2cm) and draw a light vertical line to connect them.

3 CUT OUT THE LOWER-LEFT SECTION

Cut out the lower-left section formed by the pencil line and the fold. Save this piece as a liner.

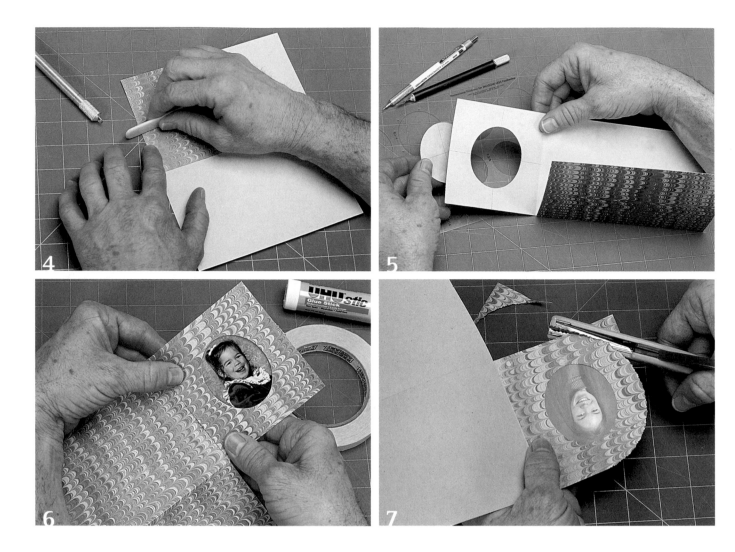

4 FOLD BACK THE SMALL FLAP

Score and crease the remaining line, then fold the left section over and crease it.

5 CUT OUT A PICTURE FRAME

Trace your desired picture shape on the inside of this top-left corner flap, then cut out the window.

6 PLACE YOUR FIRST PHOTO IN THE FRAME

Glue or tape your photo behind the frame opening. We've taped one of our niece's childhood photos in first.

7 ADD A SECOND PHOTO TO THE BACK

At this point, you can line the inside of the frame panel with the cut-out corner section. Or, as we've done, glue another photo back-to-back with the first one (the teen photo) and then glue or tape your extra panel on top to frame this inside photo. Shape the photo flap if desired.

8 WRITE YOUR LETTER AND DECORATE THE SLEEVE

Embellish and write your letter before you attach the insert to your sleeve (it's easier that way). Then, glue up the back of the top panel and adhere it to the middle section of your sleeve. Dress up your sleeve with matching decorative paper and trim the edges with decorative scissors.

DEAR GRANDMA,

8

DOUBLETAKE PHOTO IDEAS

This multifaceted foldnote offers plenty of clever possibilities. Here are a few to consider:

• Show a baby with a birthday cake followed by the child's face covered with icing.

• Insert before-and-after pictures of someone wearing a costume or makeup.

• Place a wedding photo outside and a 25th anniversary photo inside.

• Show pictures of the same house or tree in two different seasons.

If you want to take this idea a step further, glue an additional frame flap to the right side of the foldnote before gluing it into the sleeve.

★★★★★★★★★★★★★★★★★★★★

- 8½" x 11" (21.6cm x 28cm) cardstock (GRAIN SHORT), folded into a basic sleeve (SEE INSTRUCTIONS ON PAGE 64.)

- insert: 8½" x 14" (21.6cm x 35.6cm) piece of decorative paper

- bone folder

- pencil

- scissors or craft knife

- cutting mat

- glue stick or double-stick tape

- photo

- decorative paper scraps

- rubber stamps

- black ink pad

- colored pencils

Still have more photos than you know what to do with? This next frame insert is so simple that it needs no measuring. We start with a long piece of paper, so there's a generous writing surface, do a little more folding, and end up with plenty of interaction.

Folded Photo Frame

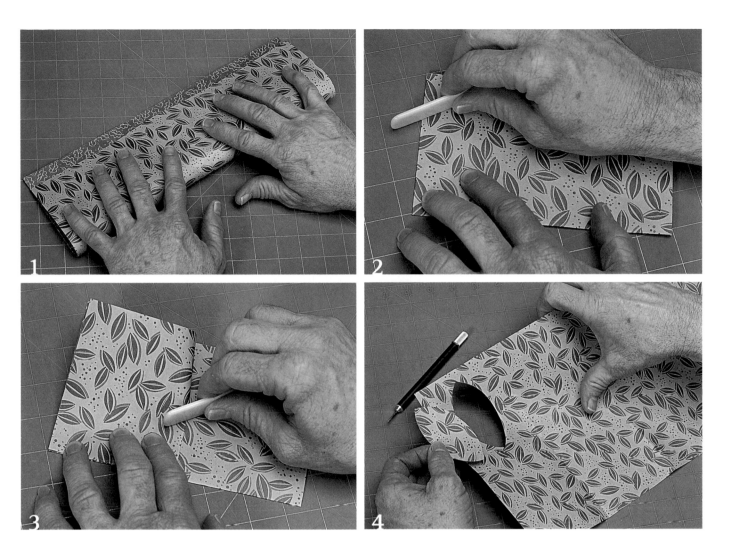

① FOLD THE BOTTOM EDGE UP

With your paper placed horizontally, fold the bottom edge to the top and crease. We chose a paper that is decorated on both sides. If only one side of your paper is decorated, start with the paper decorated side down.

② FOLD THE LEFT EDGE OVER TO THE RIGHT

Fold the left edge over to the right edge and crease.

③ FOLD THE RIGHT EDGE BACK

Now fold the right edge of the top section back to the left folded edge and crease.

④ ADD A PICTURE WINDOW

Open your paper completely, with the decorated side up, and cut out a window shape from the top-left section. Our shape mimics the shape of the leaves on our paper.

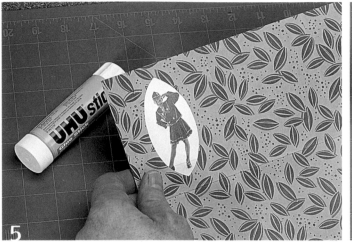

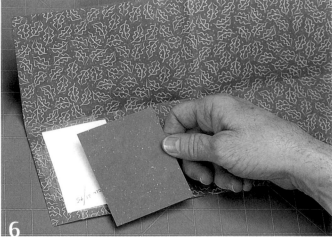

⑤ ADD A FAVORITE PHOTO
Glue or tape your photo behind the frame opening.

⑥ COVER THE BACK OF THE PHOTO
Line the back of the photo panel with contrasting or matching paper.

⑦ MAKE A COLORFUL WRITING SURFACE
If both sides of your paper are decorated, create writing surfaces by gluing in sections of paper and decorate accordingly. We're coloring in one of our favorite nature print stamps. The surprise element of this letter is the ample writing space that is revealed as the letter unfolds.

Finish by attaching the Folded Photo Frame into the center of a basic sleeve.

/ MORE FUN WITH ACCORDIONS / If one accordion fold is fun, are three accordion folds three times the fun? We think you'll have fun playing around with the possibilities for this insert. Cut all three panels the same width and stagger them as we do, or cut each one a different width, or attach them in a straight line, or turn the middle panel upside down, or have each panel open in a different direction, or... well, you get the picture.

/ A BRILLIANT IDEA / We added our own green ribbon handle to this reused accordion envelope letter. Then we tied in a mini accordion with bows and added a triangle pop-out to the bottom for a package that's full of surprises.

/ PHOTO NOT REQUIRED / The interesting thing about photo frames is that you don't have to put in a picture to get an interesting effect. Here we have used the empty frame to accent the beautiful Japanese paper behind it.

bonjour paula
thanks for the postage
stamps from paris... i
absolutely love 'em!

your letter was great.
those parisian flea mar
kets sound incroyable!

here's some
seattle paper ephemera
for your mailart
see inside

TheEnvelopePlease

Junk mail in general, and return envelopes in particular, inspired our last three projects. We've always had a hard time throwing away perfectly good gummed envelopes, even though they're preprinted with someone else's address. So, the challenge was to retain the enclosure element of the envelope and to make use of the gummed flap if possible. These envelope pockets fit the bill on both counts, and perhaps—just perhaps—collecting return envelopes will help take the edge off receiving all that unsolicited mail (well, maybe).

Like many of our correspondence projects, envelope pockets are adaptable—a favorite characteristic of ours, in case you hadn't noticed. Pick a theme for the sleeve and carry it onto the envelope pockets. Create a collage with colorful paper or images on the outside and the inside of your sleeve; hide images inside the pockets along with stamped or collaged or hand-painted notes. Cut your pockets into different lengths, angle the cut edges, number your pockets or letter them. Reuse decorated envelopes that someone else sends you, or get rid of left-over envelopes from unused holiday cards. Oh, how the mind reels! Isn't it time to decorate and send the envelope, please?!

- 8½" x 11" (21.6cm x 28cm) cardstock (GRAIN SHORT), folded into a basic sleeve (SEE INSTRUCTIONS ON PAGE 64.)
- one return envelope, approximately 8" x 4" (20.3cm x 10.2cm)
- ruler
- pencil
- bone folder
- scissors or craft knife
- cutting mat
- glue stick
- decorative paper scraps
- decorative scissors
- rubber stamps
- black ink pad

At the risk of sounding redundant, but because it bears repeating, folding is the *fun*damental step that turns paper into something more than what you see. For the Instant Envelope Pocket, we take the existing fold and reverse it, use the gummed flap to attach the envelope to a sleeve, and then dress up the plain back of the envelope—which is now the front. Got that?

Instant Envelope Pocket

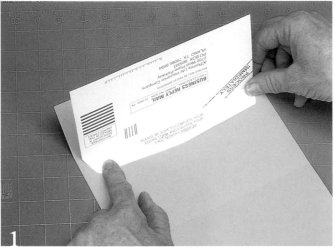

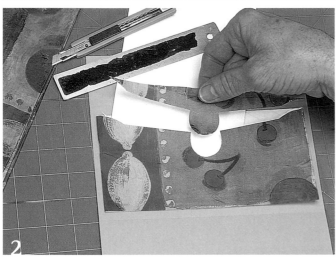

① ATTACH THE ENVELOPE TO A SLEEVE

First, make a basic sleeve out of cardstock by following the instructions on page 64. Take an envelope, open the flap and bend it backwards. Then lick the flap and use it to adhere the envelope to the middle section of your sleeve, centering it from side to side approximately 1/4" (6mm) down from the fold.

② DECORATE THE ENVELOPE

Glue decorative paper over the front surface of your envelope and trim it if necessary. Make a finger pull—a cut-out section in the front of the envelope. This finger pull is rounded, but you can make yours any shape you like.

③ DECORATE THE OUTER SLEEVE

Using images from the decorative paper, create a collage on the inside and outside of your sleeve to tie the piece together. Add collage elements to the individual note pages and stamp them with numbers to indicate the proper sequence of the correspondence.

3

HELPFUL TIP

Finger pulls are notches cut away from the front of the envelope that make it easier for you to pull out your letter. To assist you, place a piece of cardboard or tag board inside the envelope as a surface to cut against.

MaTeRiaLS NEEDED

- 8½" x 11" (21.6cm x 28cm) cardstock (GRAIN SHORT), folded into a basic sleeve (SEE INSTRUCTIONS ON PAGE 64.)

- three unused envelopes

- ruler

- pencil

- scissors or craft knife

- cutting mat

- bone folder

- glue stick

- decorative paper scraps

- rubber stamps

- black ink pad

- decorative scissors

All paper is fair game for the accordion fold, and envelopes are no exception. We use three envelopes for our Cascading Pockets, but you could easily add more. Slice off the ends to fit any size sleeve, then add decorative paper wraps to the cut ends to keep the contents in their pockets.

Cascading Envelope Pockets

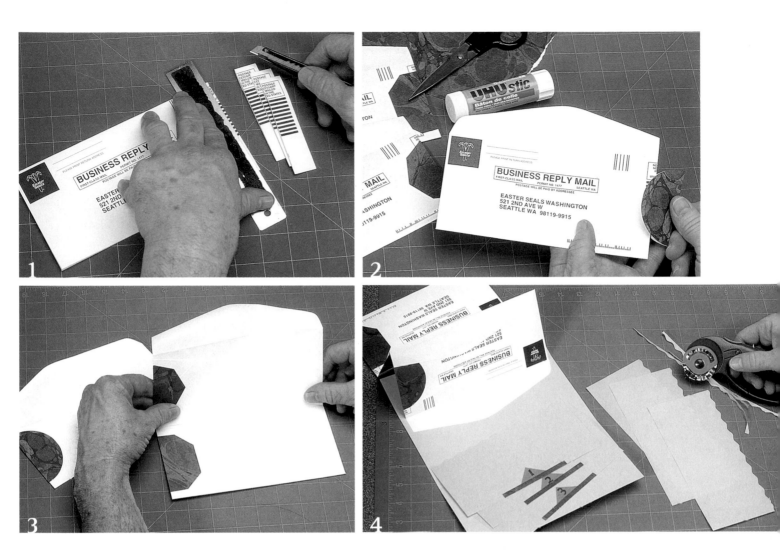

1 CUT OFF THE ENVELOPE ENDS

Many envelopes are too long to fit in a standard sleeve. To solve this problem, cut off the ends. On one envelope, measure from the left and make pencil marks at 8" (20.3cm). Then stack all three envelopes and cut off the right ends. Your envelopes will now fit the sleeve.

2 SEAL THE CUT ENDS

Open the envelope flaps. Glue decorative paper (any shape) around the open ends of each envelope to secure them.

3 CONNECT THE ENVELOPES

Lick the flap of one envelope and place the envelope on your work surface, gummed side up. Take a second envelope and lay it on top of the first envelope flap, keeping the bottom edge of the second envelope flush with the flap fold. Burnish with a bone folder. Repeat these steps for the third envelope.

4 ATTACH THE ENVELOPE POCKETS TO THE SLEEVE

Lick the remaining flap and bend it backwards, then attach the entire envelope unit to the middle section of your sleeve. Accordion fold the pockets. Your basic structure is done and ready to be decorated.

Next, make your note pages. Create greater visual interest by cutting one edge with a wavy cutter or scissors.

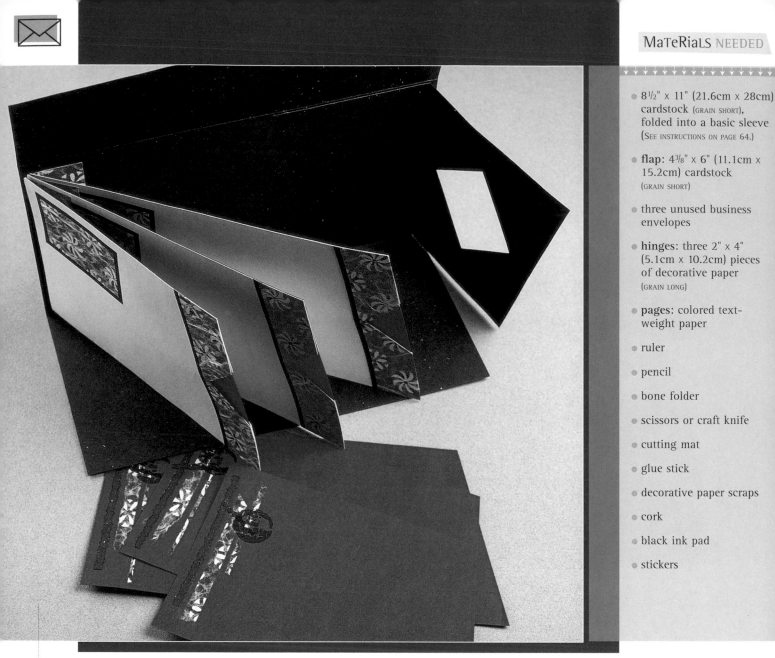

- 8½" x 11" (21.6cm x 28cm) cardstock (GRAIN SHORT), folded into a basic sleeve (SEE INSTRUCTIONS ON PAGE 64.)

- flap: 4⅜" x 6" (11.1cm x 15.2cm) cardstock (GRAIN SHORT)

- three unused business envelopes

- hinges: three 2" x 4" (5.1cm x 10.2cm) pieces of decorative paper (GRAIN LONG)

- pages: colored text-weight paper

- ruler

- pencil

- bone folder

- scissors or craft knife

- cutting mat

- glue stick

- decorative paper scraps

- cork

- black ink pad

- stickers

We've pulled out all the stops on our last project to show you just how elegant plain envelopes can be when combined with a simple sleeve, a window flap and some beautiful paper. And therein lies the true magic of creative playing around—simple combinations that create correspondence as inspiring as the person who sends it. That's *you*.

Hinged Envelope Surprise

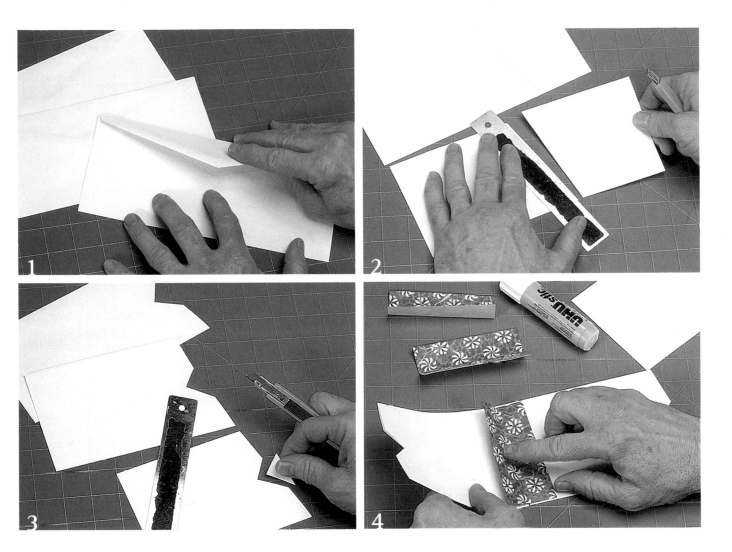

1 SEAL THE ENVELOPES

In this project, you will access the pockets from the side, not the top flap. So lick the flaps of all three envelopes, close them and burnish them with a bone folder.

2 TRIM OFF THE ENVELOPE ENDS

Cut off the right ends of your envelopes, one at 8" (20.3cm), one at 7" (17.8cm) and one at 6" (15.2cm). You can add greater visual interest by cutting the ends at an angle or rounding them.

3 CREATE THE FINGER PULLS

Cut a decorative notch out of both layers of each envelope. This finger pull will make it easier for you to remove the pages of correspondence from each pocket.

4 ATTACH THE HINGES

Fold your hinges in half lengthwise, decorative side in. Then, glue up the outside of one hinge. Place the 6" (15.2cm) and 7" (17.8cm) envelopes end to end and attach them with the hinge. Fold them together and then hinge the 8" (20.3cm) envelope to the 7" (17.8cm) envelope in the same way. Burnish the hinges flat.

⑤ ATTACH THE POCKETS TO THE SLEEVE

Glue the remaining hinge and attach the three-pocket unit to the middle section of your sleeve. Leave a ¼" (6mm) border at the left edge and center your pockets from top to bottom. Burnish the hinges with a bone folder.

⑥ CREATE THE SIDE FLAP

Next, you need to add a side flap to your sleeve. With your cardstock flap horizontal, score the inside surface 1½" (3.8cm) from the left edge, crease and fold.

⑦ ATTACH THE FLAP TO THE SLEEVE

Apply glue to the outside surface of the small section of the flap and attach the flap to the right side of your sleeve. This flap will keep pages or hundred dollar bills from falling out.

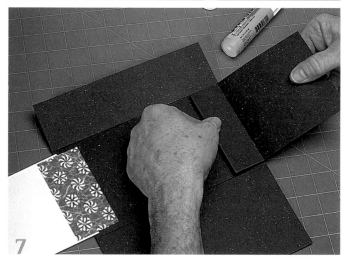

MAKING A NICER FLAP

Your side flap will open more easily if you cut your cardstock grain short, with the paper grain running parallel to the short edge of the cardstock. If you need help, see page 15 for tips on grain direction.

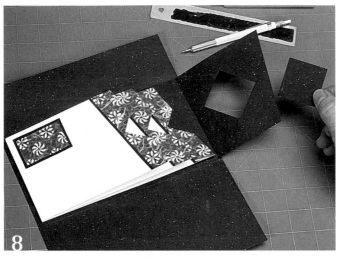

⑧ DECORATE THE POCKETS

Line the open edges of the pockets with decorative paper, then cut a window in the flap to create another layer of visual excitement.

⑨ CREATE THE INSIDE STATIONERY

Continue the oriental theme by embellishing inside pages to match. Even a simple wine cork stamped in black ink looks elegant when accented with beautiful paper strips.

⑩ ADD THE FINAL DECORATIVE TOUCHES

Finish by decorating the outer sleeve with paper scraps and a coordinating address label. No one will ever guess you started with ordinary plain envelopes when they receive your colorful, creative correspondence.

INTERESTING Variations

YO FRANCES!! to answer your question—Judy and I go out for coffee just about every day, seven days a week (are we addicted, or what?!).

Anyhoo, it's mostly at these morning coffee klatches that we brainstorm and come up with kit ideas, projects, new workshops, etc. We are happiest when we are solving creative problems.

design and work out construction techniques for 3-D projects and Judy plays with words and concepts. however, sometimes we switch roles.

We can't imagine not having fun when we work. Isn't that the way it's supposed to be? If you're having fun, then it isn't really work.

/A GIFT THAT KEEPS ON GIVING/ Looking for other ways to reuse that growing stack of used envelopes? This is an interesting twist on the Recycled Envelope Insert on page 68. Here we connect some of those envelopes in a series of hinged pages. Scraps of gift wrap make colorful hinges and perfect collage accents. It's a great way to turn waste paper into a very playful piece of correspondence.

answer
tion about
r ideas come
what about
process?

e hope this letter finds
healthy and creatively
ppy! **LOVE,**

Michael & Judy

BOOK
ART
GUILD

513 NORTH 49th

/ TROPICAL FLAVORS / This is a colorful variation on the Instant Envelope Pocket on
page 82. Instead of just one envelope, we've
stacked three envelopes cut to different lengths.
The tropical wrapping paper ties all the colors
together nicely. Finally, for more writing space,
we pasted a folded sheet of paper below.

/ CHANGING CHARACTERS / This variation on the last project shows how a change in
colors, shapes and styles can create an entirely different look. Think about giving each piece of your
creative correspondence a personality all its own.
Change the flaps, the inserts, the paper. There's
always a new combination to explore.

Resources

BOOKS

Collage Art
by Jennifer L. Atkinson
Rockport Publishers, Inc.
ISBN 1-56496-215-6

Color on Paper and Fabric:
A Wealth of Technique for
Applying Color
by Ruth Issett
Hand Books Press
ISBN 1-893164-02-0

The Crafter's Recipe Book
by Jessica Wrobel
Rockport Publishers, Inc.
ISBN 1-56496-445-0

MAGAZINES AND PERIODICALS

RubberStampMadness
P.O. Box 610
Corvallis, OR 97339-0610
(541) 752-0075
www.rsmadness.com

Somerset Studio Magazine and
Stampers' Sampler
22992 Mill Creek, Suite B
Laguna Hills, CA 92653
(949) 380-7318
(877) 782-6737
www.somersetstudio.com

Umbrella
P.O. Box 3640
Santa Monica, CA 90403
(310) 399-1146
umbrella@ix.netcom.com
• Book and mail art news and
  reviews worldwide

Expression
591 Camino de la Reina, Ste. 200
San Diego, CA 92108
(619) 819-4520
www.expressionartmagazine.com

RUBBER STAMPS AND ACCESSORIES

CLEARSNAP, INC.
P.O. Box 98
Anacortes, WA 98221
(800) 448-4862
www.clearsnap.com
• Inkpads, stamps and accessories,
  penscore

FRED B. MULLETT STAMPS
FROM NATURE PRINTS
P.O. Box 94502
Seattle, WA 98124
(206) 624-5723
www.fredbmullett.com
rbbrfish@compuserve.com

RANGER INDUSTRIES
15 Park Road
Tinton Falls, NJ 07724
(732) 389-3535
(800) 244-2111
www.rangerink.com
• Inks and accessories

RED PEARL RUBBER STAMPS
P.O. Box 94502
Seattle, WA 98124

STAMP FRANCISCO
1248 Ninth Avenue
San Francisco, CA 94122
(415) 566-1018
www.stampfrancisco.com
• Ivory Coast and Fruit Basket
  Upset rubber stamps

STEWART SUPERIOR CORP.
2050 Farallon Drive
San Leandro, CA 94577
(510) 346-9811
(800) 558-2875
www.stewartsuperior.com
• Stamp pads and accessories

TSUKINEKO
17640 NE 65th Street
Redmond, WA 98052
(425) 883-7733
(800) 769-6633
www.tsukineko.com
sales@tsukineko.com
• Stamp pads, pens and inks

TOOLS AND MATERIALS

AIKO'S ART MATERIALS
IMPORT, INC.
3347 North Clark Street
Chicago, IL 60657
(773) 404-5600
• Art supplies and Japanese papers

AMERICAN TOMBOW, INC.
2000 Newpoint Place Pkwy,
Suite 500
Lawrenceville, GA 30043
(678) 442-9224
(800) 835-3232
www.tombowusa.com
• Art supplies and pens

AMSTERDAM ART
1013 University Avenue
Berkeley, CA 94710
(510) 649-4800
• Art supplies and papers

COLOPHON BOOK ARTS SUPPLY
3611 Ryan Street SE
Lacey, WA 98503
(360) 459-2940
colophon@earthlink.com
home.earthlink.net/~colophon
• Papers, tools, binding supplies

CRAFT WORLD
(head office)
No. 8 North St., Guildford
Surrey GU1 4AF
England
07000 757070
• Retail craft stores

DANIEL SMITH FINE ARTISTS'
MATERIALS
4150 First Avenue South
P.O. Box 84268
Seattle, WA 98124-5568
(800) 426-7923
www.danielsmith.com
• Art supplies and papers

DIANE MAURER HAND
MARBLED PAPERS
P.O. Box 78
Spring Mills, PA 16875
(814) 422-8651
DKMaurer1@aol.com
• Marbling, paste paper, and
  Boku Undo dye supplies,
  decorative papers

DICK BLICK ART MATERIALS
P.O. Box 1267
Galesburg, IL 61402-1267
(800) 828-4548
www.dickblick.com
• Art supplies and papers

FEBRUARY PAPER
P.O. Box 4297
Olympia, WA 98501
(360) 330-6831
• Fibers and papers

FISKARS SCHOOL, OFFICE &
CRAFT
7811 W. Stewart Avenue
Wausau, WI 54401
(800) 950-0203
www.fiskars.com
• Scissors and paper cutters

HOBBY CRAFTS
(head office)
River Court, Southern Sector
Bournemouth International
Airport
Christ Church
Dorset BH23 6SE
England
0800 272387
• Retail craft stores

JOHN NEAL, BOOKSELLER
1833 Spring Garden Street
Greensboro, NC 27403
(336) 272-6139
(800) 369-9598
www.johnnealbooks.com
info@johnnealbooks.com
• Books, tools and calligraphy
  supplies

LA PAPETERIE ST. ARMAND
3700 St. Patrick
Montreal, Quebec
H4E 1A2 Canada
(514) 931-8338
• Papermaking supplies

MARVY-UCHIDA
3535 Del Amo Blvd.
Torrance, CA 90503
(800) 541-5877
www.uchida.com
• Markers, dye inks and supplies

NASCO ARTS & CRAFTS
4825 Stoddard Road
P.O. Box 3837
Modesto, CA 95356-3837
(800) 558-9595
www.enasco.com
info@nascofa.com
• Huge selection of art materials
  and tools

NEW YORK CENTRAL ART
SUPPLY
62 Third Avenue
New York, NY 10003
(212) 477-0400
(800) 950-6111
www.nycentralart.com
• Art supplies

THE ORIGINAL PAPER-YA
9-1666 Johnston Street
Granville Island,
Vancouver, BC
V6H 3S2 Canada
(604) 684-2531
• Papers

PAM BAKKE PASTE PAPERS
303 Highland Drive
Bellingham, WA 98225
(360) 738-4830
• Hand-decorated papers

PAPER & INK ARTS
3 North Second Street
Woodsboro, MD 21798
(800) 736-7772
www.paperinkarts.com
• Art and calligraphy supplies,
  papers, tools and books

PAPER SOURCE, INC.
232 W Chicago Avenue
Chicago, IL 60610
(312) 337-0798
• Papers

PEARL PAINT CO. INC.
308 Canal Street
New York, NY 10013-2572
(800) 221-6845
www.pearlpaint.com
• Art supplies and papers

SKYCRAFT DESIGNS, INC.
26395 S. Morgan Road
Estacada, OR 97023
(503) 630-7173
(800) 578-5608
www.skycraft.com
peggy@skycraft.com
• Hand-decorated papers and
  supplies

THINK INK
7526 Olympic View Drive, Suite E
Edmonds, WA 98026-5556
(425) 778-1935
(800) 778-1935
• Gocco Printing Supplies

USARTQUEST, INC.
7800 Ann Arbor Road
Grass Lake, MI 49240
(517) 522-6225
(800) 200-7848
www.usartquest.com
• Unique art materials, Perfect
  Paper Adhesive

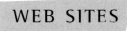

WEB SITES

www.silverfoxstamps.com
• Huge listing of rubber stamp
  stores in the U.S.

www.thecreativezone.com
• Papercraft kits, book arts and
  papercraft workshops throughout the U.S.

www.art-e-zine.co.uk
/artemalluk.html
• Listing of rubber stamp suppliers
  in the United Kingdom.

Index

STAMP CREDITS

p. 1 Alphabet—Ivory Coast

p. 3 Cat—Fruit Basket Upset
This is recycled paper—M. Jacobs

p. 4 Man—clip art
Alphabet—hand-carved

p. 5 Love, ship—Fruit Basket Upset

p. 6 Woman's face, mail man—Fruit Basket
Upset
Banner Postcard—Stamp Francisco
Cancellation mark, 3-d kinda guy,
cowboy and cowgirl—personal stamps
of M. Jacobs

p. 7 Divine, disgusting, unofficial, cancellation marks, acrobats—personal
stamps of M. Jacobs
Dear mom!—Fruit Basket Upset
Arrow, genuine—clip art

p. 20 Hi—Ivory Coast
All other alphabets—Fruit Basket Upset
Banner Postcard—Stamp Francisco
Man head, arrow—clip art

p. 21 Clown—clip art

p. 22 Banner Postcard—Stamp Francisco
Cat, yin/yang, Yo!—Fruit Basket Upset
Postcard, cancellation mark, star,
Howdy—personal stamps of M. Jacobs
Man head, little guy—clip art

p. 24 Hey Howdy, Love, texture stamp—
Fruit Basket Upset
Hi!—Ivory Coast
Greetings, A and B—Rubberstampede
Cancellation marks, arrow—personal
stamps of M. Jacobs

p. 26 alphabet letters—Fruit Basket Upset
3-D kinda guy, unofficial, arrows, man
head—personal stamps of M. Jacobs

p. 30 Yo!—Fruit Basket Upset
Numbers—Ivory Coast

p. 35 Cat, Yo, Sandra—Fruit Basket Upset
Yo!—Rubberstampede

p. 36 Hey Howdy—Fruit Basket Upset
Symbols—Ivory Coast

p. 37 Clown—Fruit Basket Upset

p. 43 Alphabet, numbers—Fruit Basket Upset

p. 46 cowboys and cowgirl—personal stamps
of M. Jacobs

p. 47 A and B—Ivory Coast

p. 48 Hello—Ivory Coast
Pen, inkspot, worlds, ornate square—
Fruit Basket Upset

p. 53 Decorative stamps—Fruit Basket Upset

p. 56 Alphabet—Ivory Coast
Nature print—Fred B. Mullett

p. 58 Hello—Ivory Coast
Worlds, shell—Fruit Basket Upset

p. 60 Ship—Fruit Basket Upset

p. 61 Howdy—personal stamps of M. Jacobs
1 and 4, address, Oh Yes, jester—Fruit
Basket Upset
Take time to play—hand-carved

p. 62 Yo Betsy—hand-carved
Dear Grandma—Ivory Coast

p. 63 Clown—Fruit Basket Upset
Asian stamp used as a pattern—
Red Pearl

p. 64 Cancellation mark—personal stamps of
M. Jacobs

p. 68 Alphabet—hand-carved
Fish—Fred B. Mullett

p. 70 Alphabet—hand-carved
Zen master, arrow, pointing man,
acrobats—personal stamps of M. Jacobs

p. 72 Dear Grandma—Ivory Coast

p. 78 Nature print—Fred B. Mullett

p. 79 Bonjour paula—Ivory Coast
One, Two, Three—personal stamps of
M. Jacobs

p. 80 Numbers—Ivory Coast

p. 84 a, b, c—hand-carved
1, 2, 3—Ivory Coast

p. 90 Yo Frances!, love—Ivory Coast
Couple by campfire—Fruit Basket Upset

Get Creative

with North Light Books!

The Essential Guide to Handmade Books

Gabrielle Fox teaches you how to create your own handmade books—one-of-a-kind art pieces that go beyond the standard definition of what a book can be. You'll find 11 projects inside. Each one builds upon the next, just as your skills increase. This beginner-friendly progression ensures that you're well prepared to experiment, play and design your own unique handmade books. ISBN 1-58180-019-3, paperback, 128 pages, #31652-K

THE ESSENTIAL GUIDE TO MAKING
HANDMADE Books
Easy-to-follow instructions for 11 timeless binding techniques, plus 58 unique variations
Gabrielle Fox

How to Be Creative if You Never Thought You Could
Let Tera Leigh act as your personal craft guide and motivator. She'll help you discover just how creative you really are. You'll explore eight exciting crafts through 16 fun, fabulous projects, including rubber stamping, book-making, papermaking, collage, decorative painting and more. Tera prefaces each new activity with insightful essays and encouraging advice. ISBN 1-58180-293-5, paperback, 128 pages, #32170-K

how to be **creative** if you never thought you could
Tera Leigh

Greeting Card Magic with Rubber Stamps
Discover great new tricks for creating extra-special greeting cards! Pick up your stamp, follow along with the illustrated, step-by-step directions inside, and ta da!—you'll amaze everyone (including yourself!) with your beautiful and original creations. ISBN 0-89134-979-0, paperback, 128 pages, #31521-K

greeting card magic with RUBBER STAMPS
Mary Jo McGraw author of Making Greeting Cards With Rubber Stamps

Making Greeting Cards with Rubber Stamps
Here are hundreds of colorful ideas and techniques for creating one-of-a-kind greet-ings—from the elegant to the festive to the downright goofy—all in a matter of minutes! Try your hand at any of the 30 step-by-step projects inside or take off in your own original direction. ISBN 0-89134-713-5, paperback, 128 pages, #30821-K

MAKING **Greeting Cards** WITH **Rubber Stamps**
MARY JO McGRAW

These and other fine North Light titles are available from your local art or craft retailer, bookstore, online supplier or by calling 1-800-448-0915.